Collins

WITHDRAWN

A Bridge to GCSE English
Student Book

English
English Language
English Literature

Sarah Darragh
Phil Darragh
John Parry

William Collins' dream of knowledge for all began with the publication of his first book in 1819. A self-educated mill worker, he not only enriched millions of lives, but also founded a flourishing publishing house. Today, staying true to this spirit, Collins books are packed with inspiration, innovation and practical expertise. They place you at the centre of a world of possibility and give you exactly what you need to explore it.

Collins. Freedom to teach.

Published by Collins
An imprint of HarperCollins Publishers
77–85 Fulham Palace Road
Hammersmith
London
W6 8JB

Browse the complete Collins catalogue at
www.collinseducation.com

© HarperCollins Publishers Limited 2011

10 9 8 7 6 5 4 3 2 1
ISBN 978 0 00 741595 3

Phil Darragh, Sarah Darragh and John Parry assert their moral rights to be identified as the authors of this work.

British Library Cataloguing in Publication Data.
A Catalogue record for this publication is available from the British Library.

Commissioned by Catherine Martin
Edited and project-managed by Tim Satterthwaite
Design and typesetting by Jordan Publishing Design Limited
Cover Design by Angela English
Picture research by Caroline Green
Printed and bound by Printing Express

With particular thanks to Gudrun Kaiser and Jackie Newman.

Acknowledgements

The publishers gratefully acknowledge the permissions granted to reproduce the copyright material in this book. While every effort has been made to trace and contact copyright holders, where this has not been possible the publishers will be pleased to make the necessary arrangements at the first opportunity.

Chapter 1 pp6, 10 extracts from *Flying Upside Down* by Malcolm Rose, published by Scholastic. Reprinted with permission; p18 from *Americana* by Don DeLillo © 1971 by Don DeLillo. Published by Penguin Group USA. Used with permission of the Wallace Literary Agency, Inc; p20 extract from *The Whole Town's Sleeping* by Ray Bradbury, published by McCalls © 1950, renewed 1977 by Ray Bradbury. Reprinted with permission of Don Congdon Associates, Inc.

Chapter 2 p40 extract from *The Silence of the Lambs* by Thomas Harris, published by William Heinemann. Used with permission of The Random House Group Ltd; p46 extract from *To Kill a Mockingbird* by Harper Lee, published by William Heinemann. Reprinted with permission of The Random House Group Ltd and Aitken Alexander Associates. **Chapter 3** p56 'The Storm' by Asokbijay Raha, translated from the Bengali by Lila Ray, from *The Beloit Poetry Journal Vol. 13, Number 2, Winter 1962–63*; p58 'Below the Green Corrie' by Norman MacCaig from The Poems of Norman MacCaig edited by Ewen MacCaig, published by Polygon © 2005. Reproduced with permission from Polygon, an imprint of Birlinn Ltd; p65 'A Day in Autumn' by R. S. Thomas, from *Poetry for Supper* Rupert Hart Davis, 1958 © Kunjana Thomas 2001. Reprinted with permission; p66 'Nettles' By Vernon Scannell, from *The Very Best of Vernon Scannell* published by Macmillan, 2001, reprinted with permission of Mr. Martin Reed, Literary executor to the estate of Vernon Scannell; p67 'Thistles' by Ted Hughes, from *Selected Poems 1957–61*. Published by Faber and Faber; p70 'Storm on the Island' by Seamus Heaney, from *Death of a Naturalist*. Published by Faber and Faber; p75 'Winter Swans' by Owen Sheets, from *Skirrid Hill*, published by Seren Books © 2006 Owen Sheers. Reproduced with permission of the author c/o Rogers Coleridge & White Ltd. **Chapter 5** p109 extract and artwork © Crown Copyright material reproduced with the permission of the Controller HMSO; p110 extract from *The First-time Cook* by Sophie Grigson. Published by Collins, part of HarperCollins *Publishers*. Reprinted with permission; p114 from 'Beauty: An endearingly quaint advertising scandal' by Lucy Mangan from *The Guardian*, 7 January 2010 © Guardian News & Media Ltd 2010; p123 extract from *The Road to Wigan Pier* by George Orwell © George Orwell, 1937. Reprinted with permission of Bill Hamilton as the Literary Executor of the Estate of the Late Sonia Brownell Orwell and Secker & Warburg Ltd; p124 'Supposing … you are not what you eat' by Charlie Brooker from *The Guardian*, 6 October, 2006 © Guardian News & Media Ltd 2006. Used with permission; p126 'Glossy magazines face air brush ban' by Sophie Borland from *The Telegraph*, 2 April 2008. Reprinted with permission. **Chapter 6** p140 extract from Monty Python Argument Sketch. Reprinted with kind permission of Monty (Python) Pictures. **Chapter 7** p163 *Radio Times* interview with Emma Thompson; p164 'Does slang make you sound stupid?' by Robert McCrum and Doc Brown from *The Observer* 3 October 2010; p169 transcript from Racing Commentary 14.55 Thirsk Saturday, 4th September, 2010 Channel 4 (2010). Reprinted with permission of Channel Four Television Corporation; pp170–171 transcript from Sky Sports Commentary on MK Dons v Hartlepool, Saturday, 4th September, 2010. Reprinted with kind permission of Sky Sports.

The publishers would like to thank the following for permission to reproduce pictures in these pages:

Advertising Archives: pp109, 120(l), 125. **Alamy**: pp2, 12, 14, 37, 55, 61, 83, 86, 87, 92–93, 94–95, 99, 101, 106, 107, 115(t), 132, 133, 140–1, 146–7, 155, 164–5, 171. **Bridgeman Art Library**: pp85, 90–91. **Getty Images**: p144–5. **iStockphoto**: pp16, 28–29, 159. **Mary Evans Picture Library**: p122. **Photos.com**: p42(t). **Rex Features**: pp40, 44, 46, 89, 163, 169, 170, 173, 174. **Shutterstock**: 2(tl), 3, 5, 6, 7, 9, 10, 11, 22, 32, 35, 42(b), 47, 56, 58, 62(l), 62(r), 65, 66, 67, 68, 69, 71, 74, 75, 78, 88, 100, 102–3, 108, 110, 110–11, 112, 115(b), 117(t), 117(b), 124, 134–5, 136, 137, 138(t), 138(b), 139, 142, 148, 150–1, 154, 157, 157(r), 158, 160, 161, 162, 166–7. **Splash News and Pictures**: p126. **TopFoto**: pp82, 84, 96–97.

Contents

Chapter 1

Writing creative texts

In this chapter you will be writing an imaginative opening to a mystery story. You will learn how to choose vocabulary and shape sentences and paragraphs carefully so that your writing has maximum impact on the reader. You will also be shown how to build suspense by using the 'show, don't tell' technique.

Bridge to GCSE

To get you ready for your GCSE course, this chapter will take you through the following steps:

Explore ideas
- Learn from other writers about the craft of creative writing.
- Craft your writing deliberately and effectively to create a strong mood and atmosphere and to hook your reader.

Check your skills
- Experiment with different types of sentence to create different effects.

Extend your skills
- Build sentences into well-structured paragraphs for variety and impact.

Plan and write
- Plan a piece of creative writing and create a 'notes page'.
- Complete this writing task under controlled conditions.

Improve your work
- Review your response and set yourself a target for improvement.

Your GCSE-style assessment task will be to write the first chapter of a mystery story.

**Key Stage 3
Writing Assessment Focuses**

AF1 Write imaginative, interesting and thoughtful texts

AF3 Organise and present whole texts effectively, sequencing and structuring information, ideas and events

AF5 Vary sentences for clarity, purpose and effect

AF7 Select appropriate and effective vocabulary

**GCSE English/English Language
Assessment Objectives**

AO3/4i Write to communicate clearly, effectively and imaginatively, using and adapting forms and selecting vocabulary [...] in ways that engage the reader

AO3/4ii Organise [...] ideas into structured and sequenced sentences, paragraphs and whole texts [...]

Beginning the story

Learning objective

- To explore the ways that writers engage the reader's interest at the start of a story.
- To use interesting descriptive vocabulary to create atmosphere.

Bridge to GCSE

- At GCSE you will need to show that you can engage the reader by deliberately choosing language to create a specific atmosphere and mood.

A good writer knows that the first few lines of their story need to grab the attention of the reader. The opening needs to make the reader want to read on and find out more. Thinking about how to interest your reader is an important skill to develop for GCSE.

Getting you thinking

Flying Upside Down, by Malcolm Rose, is a crime thriller. Glynn, the central character, has to uncover the mystery of what led to the death of his friend Duncan.

Look at the very first paragraph. How does Rose get us interested in the story?

In one corner of the ceiling a spider, caught unexpectedly in the torch light, scurried into a crack in the dilapidated brickwork. Further along the wall, rain seeped through gaps in the mortar and dribbled down the masonry like blood from a wound. The shaft of light followed the watercourse downwards, causing the green algae growing in the stream to glisten. The damp patch disappeared behind a corroded contraption that had once been mounted on a wagon as a mobile winch. Underneath it, a pool of rust-red water had probably collected. The beam swept along to a stack of tarred wooden sleepers, but lingered for a moment on the three candles that had been wedged securely on top. Wax, long since solidified, had cascaded liberally down each one, indicating considerable use. Continuing its exploration of the dank room, the circle of light probed discarded girders, a bucket of hardcore and coal dust that was alive with woodlice, old pipework, a broken spade and, finally, the door that should have been sealed.

1 What kind of tone and atmosphere do you think Malcolm Rose is trying to create?

2 Either on your own, or with a partner, make a list of the vocabulary he uses to create this kind of atmosphere.

3 Writers often create tension by making the reader wait – in other words, by deliberately holding back vital information. Notice, for example, how

- a torch beam is mentioned but we do not know who is holding the torch
- we are not told where the setting is – we have to work it out from the things the torch beam picks out
- little clues are used to create 'hooks'.

Discuss with a partner what the following two clues might suggest about the story, setting or characters.

a 'Wax, long since solidified, had cascaded liberally down each one, indicating considerable use.'

b '…the door that should have been sealed.'

Top tip

Although adjectives and adverbs add extra descriptive detail, the power of well-chosen verbs should not be ignored. Verbs are the 'power houses' of really effective creative writing.

GCSE skills focus

Adverbs and adjectives help a writer to paint a picture in the reader's mind by adding extra information.

- **Adjectives** can add extra information to **nouns** (people, places, objects).
- **Adverbs** can add extra information to **verbs** (movements, actions, states of being).

Key terms

Synonym A word which means the same as another word.

    noun   verb   noun
The man walked across the road.

   adjectives   verb   adverb   adjectives
The small, grey figure of a man shuffled dejectedly across the heaving, traffic-choked road.

Notice how using a **synonym** for the verb 'walked' adds extra meaning to the sentence, as do the adjectives and adverb.

By altering the verb, adjectives and adverb, we can totally change the meaning and mood of the sentence:

        adjectives   verb   adverb   adjectives

*The small, grey **figure** of a man **shuffled** dejectedly across the heaving, traffic-choked **road**.*

        adjectives   verb   adverb   adjectives

*The small, sprightly **figure** of a man **skipped** nimbly across the vibrant, bustling **road**.*

- Compare the two sentences. Can you describe the mood in each one? In what way are the moods different?

Now you try it

1 Here are three new basic sentences for you to improve by choosing more imaginative vocabulary.

In pairs, take each sentence in turn and improve them by selecting more interesting words.

Write out each sentence twice, creating a negative mood the first time and a positive mood the second time.

a The dog barked as the man walked through the door.

b A flock of birds flew into the air.

c The mother looked at her child.

2 Interesting and varied vocabulary can lift your creative writing to a high level.

Think of some interesting alternatives to the words below.

Obvious word	More interesting alternative
Dirty	Grimy / filthy / squalid
Looked at	Observed / scrutinised / scanned
Dark	
Empty	
Moved slowly	
Untidy	
Quiet	

Top tip

Think about
- using more precise nouns and verbs
- using adverbs to add more information to the verb(s)
- inserting some interesting adjectives to describe the noun(s).

Bridge to GCSE

A thesaurus could help with this activity, but be sure you understand the meaning of the word you choose.

The key to success is selecting precise vocabulary that relates to the overall atmosphere you are trying to create.

Taking it further

Practise using these techniques, and your interesting vocabulary choices, by writing the first paragraph of your own story called 'The Watcher'.

- You are going to describe somebody watching an empty house through binoculars.
- You cannot say who the person holding the binoculars is, or who the house belongs to.
- You should try to describe the house and its surroundings 'through the binoculars'.

One student used this first sentence:

> The blurred image of a cracked and dusty window came slowly into sharp focus through the lens of the binoculars...

Checklist for success

✓ Write in the third person using 'he' or 'she' to refer to characters.

✓ Write in the past tense and maintain it.

✓ Try to include some descriptive language (adverbs and adjectives) to add layers of interest.

✓ Use powerful, well-chosen verbs.

✓ Focus on small details to add to the overall picture.

Top tip

See if you can subtly include some clues to suggest the identity of the watcher or perhaps why they are watching the house.

What have you learnt?

Read your paragraph. Highlight where you have:

- hinted or referred to the binoculars
- mentioned interesting details to suggest that the house is empty and mysterious
- created a menacing atmosphere
- used interesting vocabulary choices to affect the atmosphere.

Bridge to GCSE

You will have time during your controlled assessment period to check over your work, editing and adapting as you go. If you get used to developing your skills as an editor now, you will be an expert by GCSE.

Check your level

LEVEL 5 I can structure my writing clearly and choose vocabulary to create different tones and atmospheres.

LEVEL 6 I can shape my writing and choose ambitious vocabulary to create tone and atmosphere.

LEVEL 7 I can skilfully shape my writing and choose imaginative vocabulary well matched to my purpose.

Learning objective

- To develop the skill of 'show, don't tell' to make your story interesting for the reader.
- To keep the reader interested with your choice of vocabulary.

Bridge to GCSE

- At GCSE you will be assessed on your ability to use a wider range of interesting vocabulary for effect.

Every word counts in creative writing. Being deliberate and precise with the words you choose can have a powerful effect on the quality of your work. Learning to play with language to create deliberate effects is one of the most important skills you can develop for GCSE.

Getting you thinking

Read the next three paragraphs from the first chapter of *Flying Upside Down*. What do you think is 'going on' here? Can you describe Glynn's mood and feelings from the clues the writer gives us?

> Glynn turned off the torch and leaned back against the cold, squalid wall. He could hear a faint scrabbling noise somewhere to his left. Probably the claws of a rat on concrete. He ignored the sound. 'So this is it,' he said sadly to himself. 'Duncan's bolt-hole. This is where he would have come if he hadn't...' The wall reverberated as an interminable goods train lumbered past the grim sanctuary. Grim perhaps – but, to Duncan, it would have been heaven. 'If only, after what he did for me, I'd...'
>
> Tormented by conscience, Glynn sighed and shut his eyes in the vain hope of preventing tears of anguish. Standing there in the dark, he felt as if he were entombed. Or maybe a desecrator of someone else's tomb. He sighed again. He was not sure that he still had the appetite to search Duncan's refuge for the treasure that he knew Duncan had hidden in it, but he didn't really have a choice. He had to find it.
>
> To put off the task for a short while, Glynn replayed in his mind the events of the last two weeks.

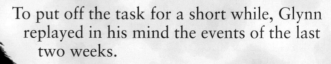

1 In this section, the writer gives many clues to the state of mind of the central character, Glynn. Either working on your own or with a partner, identify and copy out the words and phrases used by the writer to reveal Glynn's state of mind.

2 Copy and complete the table below. Your task is to explain clearly how the writer's choice of language gives subtle hints and suggestions about Glynn's state of mind.

At the end of the table add some evidence of your own and comment on it.

🔑 **Key terms**

Implies The writer gives subtle clues rather than obvious statements so the reader must 'read between the lines' to tease out the meaning.

Sibilant Repetition of 's' sound for deliberate atmospheric/tonal effect.

Clue	What this tells us
'Glynn…leaned back against the cold, squalid wall.'	**Implies**…
'He ignored the sound.'	Suggests that…
'Glynn sighed and shut his eyes'	Suggests that there is something he doesn't want to acknowledge or 'look at'. His sigh suggests he is overcome by the thought of the task ahead. Sibilant quality of the phrase highlights the strength of Glynn's 'sigh'.
'in the vain hope of preventing tears of anguish'	Highlights …

GCSE skills focus

'Show, don't tell' involves *demonstrating* a character's emotions rather than simply telling the reader about them. Read the following sentences and decide which of the suggested emotions they demonstrate to you.

a *The watcher clenched her fists tightly until her knuckles shone white.*

b *She took a series of deep, calming breaths.*

c *Another glance at her watch; the fourth in as many minutes.*

     Anxiety   **Impatience**   **Anger**

What other emotions might these sentences suggest?

Good writers allow their readers to work out what is going on rather than simply telling them. They imply meaning and suggest ideas and feelings. Your writing can be just as subtle and interesting if you 'show, don't tell'.

Now you try it

Think about the following three emotions:

● relief
● joy
● determination.

How might a person look or behave if they were experiencing these emotions?

● Write a sentence from your story 'The Watcher' using each of the three emotions in turn. You must show the emotion without actually mentioning it, as in the examples above. See how subtle and interesting you can make your sentences.

Top tip

If you are writing in the **third person** you should try to 'show' a character's emotions through description rather than 'telling' the reader how the character is feeling.

Taking it further

Pathetic fallacy is the term for a technique used by many writers, in which the things around us (the natural world) echo and mirror the atmosphere of the story or the character's feelings.

Here are two examples of pathetic fallacy:

> As she ran into the forest, fingers of branches clawed viciously at her from all directions.

> When he woke from his fitful dreams in the morning, the frost had drawn crazy patterns across the bedroom window.

You can use descriptive language deliberately to create the right mood. For example:

> The wind blew into him and reminded him of what he had to do.

can become…

> A sudden icy blast of wind bit savagely through his jacket, tearing him from his dark thoughts and focusing his mind with a fierce determination.

1 Write a sentence of your own using pathetic fallacy, to convey one of the three emotions: relief, joy, determination. Aim to create a definite mood through precise descriptions of the weather, the time of day, or nature.

2 Continue the story of 'The Watcher' from the first paragraph you wrote in the previous section. Your task is to gradually reveal some information about the character with the binoculars. You need to make sure that you 'show, don't tell'.

Either with a partner or as a group, discuss your ideas about the following questions:

- What does the watcher look like?
- Who or what are they waiting for?
- Why are they watching?
- Where are they?
- How are they feeling?

What have you learnt?

1 Work with a partner. Choose a sentence from the section you have just written which you think gives the reader a clue about your 'watcher'. Read the sentence to your partner and see what they can work out from your writing. Can they work out how your character is feeling?

2 Now do the same with your partner's work – what can you work out about their character from a sentence in their writing?

3 What did you think? Were the clues too obvious or too hard? Could you and your partner have made your writing more interesting? Write each other a comment which picks out something they have done well.

Check your level

LEVEL 5 I can choose vocabulary for effect.

LEVEL 6 I can carefully choose vocabulary for deliberate effect on my reader.

LEVEL 7 I can skilfully choose imaginative vocabulary that provides clues about my characters.

Learning objective

● To explore ways of writing different types of sentence.

Bridge to GCSE

● At GCSE you will be assessed on your use of sentences for effect and purpose.

You already know that it is important to use clear and accurate sentences in your writing. However, being able to use different types of sentences deliberately for effect will dramatically improve the quality of your writing. If you can vary the length and style of the sentences in your writing it will be much more interesting to read. This is one of the main techniques you can learn, to improve the rhythm and pace of a story.

Getting you thinking

Do you know what the three main sentence types are?

A **simple sentence** consists of one *clause*, which means one main **verb** and usually one **subject**. Simple sentences are useful for emphasising particular or important details. They can alter the pace of the writing – slowing it down or creating suspense and shock.

> '*The dog lay outside in the sunshine'*.
>   Subject   Verb

A **compound sentence** consists of two independent clauses or simple sentences, connected with a **connective** (and, but, or). Compound sentences link important ideas together and can be used to alter pace or direction:

> '*The dog lay outside in the sunshine but the cat stayed indoors.'*
>   Subject   Verb   Connective

A **complex sentence** consists of one **main clause** with one or more **subordinate clauses**. Complex sentences enable writers to describe precisely and in detail, using extra clauses to add shades of meaning. The different clauses are separated by commas:

> 'The dog, who was very tired, lay outside in the sunshine.
>
> 'The dog lay outside in the sunshine, dreaming of cats.
>   Main clause   Subordinate clause

Key terms

Subject The person or thing doing the action.

Verb A 'doing' or 'being' word.

Connective Words used to link or join ideas or clauses together.

Main clause The key part of the sentence, which makes sense by itself.

Subordinate clause Adds information to the main clause and is dependent on it. Separated from the main clause by commas, it cannot stand alone.

The following short passage uses a mixture of simple, compound and complex sentences.

● Pick out one simple, one compound and one complex sentence from the passage.

The dog lay outside in the sunshine. It was a hot day so he panted as he lay there. There was no breeze. A cat, cautious and cunning, slowly edged towards him. She moved like a panther. She stepped carefully forwards, black and silky, moving through the grass like she was in the jungle. The dog stirred and opened his eyes briefly but went back to sleep straight away. He whined in his sleep, flexing his legs as if chasing an invisible squirrel.

The cat froze, then darted for the safety of a nearby tree.

Jumping up suddenly, the dog woke up as he heard the voice of his owner from inside the house. He padded slowly inside.

GCSE skills focus

Simple sentences can be used for clarity or emphasis.

Complex sentences can add extra detail and make your writing interesting and thoughtful.

Look at this example:

Top tip

A well-placed simple sentence can draw the reader's attention to something surprising. It can be shocking, or amusing.

Simple sentence: *The sun rose over the deserted beach.*

Complex sentence A: *Casting a golden light, the sun rose over the deserted beach.*

Complex sentence B: *The sun, creating long shadows as it appeared, rose over the deserted beach.*

Complex sentence C: *The sun rose over the deserted beach, empty and golden in the morning light.*

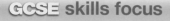

Main clause   Subordinate clause

Notice how you can place subordinate clauses at the beginning, end or in the middle of a complex sentence.

Also, notice the use of commas. Remember, subordinate clauses are always separated from the main clause by commas.

Now you try it

Have a look at the three simple sentences below. Using the information on the previous page, turn each **simple** sentence into a **complex** sentence. Try to put your subordinate clauses in different places each time, as in the examples on page 15.

a The class waited for their teacher.

b The crowd gathered outside the stadium.

c The town centre was packed with shoppers.

Taking it further

Look at this example of a first paragraph from 'The Watcher' written by a student.

The binoculars gradually focused on a cracked and dusty window. A spider hung from a thin silken thread. It looked like a tiny gust of wind would blow it away. The binoculars moved slightly to the left. Now they were looking at another window. This time the window was broken. Now the watcher could see inside the house. The window was downstairs. It was probably the dining room window. The watcher could see a sideboard and a dining table. They were covered in dust and cobwebs. There was a newspaper on the sideboard. The watcher zoomed in on the newspaper. It showed yesterday's date. So the house was inhabited after all.

Bridge to GCSE

One third of the available marks for writing at GCSE are awarded for sentence structure, spelling and accurate, well-used punctuation.

1 Rewrite the paragraph, adapting the sentences until you have a range of simple and complex sentences.

You may want to add some subordinate clauses or join two simple sentences together to make one **complex sentence**.

You may also decide to add some extra details and interesting vocabulary to make the writing even more effective.

Try using just one **simple sentence** for effect, perhaps at the end.

2 Paragraphs are used to break up the text into sections. Each paragraph develops an idea, or moves a story forward. Start a new paragraph to show a

- change of subject
- change of location
- change of time
- change of person speaking.

Bridge to GCSE

Making strong links between your paragraphs, structuring and sequencing them, is one way of showing that you are crafting your writing deliberately. This will raise your grade at GCSE.

Each paragraph should connect to the paragraph before in a logical way, so that the reader can follow the direction of the story.

- Look at the three paragraphs from *Flying Upside Down* on page 10. Working with a partner, decide why you think the author chose to break up the story in this way.

What have you learnt?

1 Highlight where you have used complex sentences in your own work.

2 Circle the commas you have used to separate the clauses in your complex sentences.

3 Write down the difference between a simple and a complex sentence.

4 Write a sentence explaining two reasons for using complex sentences.

Swap your ideas with your partner. Did you both have similar points?

Check your level	**LEVEL 4**	I can write accurate sentences with correctly placed full stops and commas.
	LEVEL 5	I can use a variety of sentence types and length.
	LEVEL 6	I can use a variety of simple and complex sentences to contribute to the overall effect.

Learning objective

- To consider ways of shaping a variety of sentence types for effect.
- To think about building sentences into effective paragraphs.

Bridge to GCSE

- At GCSE you will need to demonstrate that you can manipulate paragraphs to craft, structure and organise your writing.

Different sentence types can be used for different purposes and effects. If you can deliberately use a range and variety of simple, compound and complex sentences to create paragraphs it will add depth and interest to your writing.

Getting you thinking

Read the first paragraph of *Americana* by Don DeLillo.

It is written in the **first-person narrative voice**. The novel is set at Christmas time in New York. The narrator is a successful and well-paid television executive who is bored with his job and is struggling to find meaning in his life.

 Key terms

First-person narrative voice
When the story is told from the perspective of one character, in their voice, using 'I'.

Then we came to the end of another dull and lurid year. Lights were strung across the front of every shop. Men selling chestnuts wheeled their smoky carts. In the evenings the crowds were immense and traffic built to a tidal roar. The santas of Fifth Avenue rang their little bells with an odd sad delicacy, as if sprinkling salt on some brutally spoiled piece of meat. Music came from all the stores in jingles, chants and hosannas, and from the Salvation Army bands came the martial trumpet lament of ancient Christian legions. It was a strange sound to hear in that time and place, the smack of cymbals and high-collared drums, a suggestion that children were being scolded for a bottomless sin, and it seemed to annoy people. But the girls were lovely and undismayed, shopping in every mad store, striding through those magnetic twilights like drum majorettes, tall and pink, bright packages cradled to their tender breasts. The blind man's German shepherd slept through it all.

Simple sentences
Compound sentences
Complex sentences

1 What do you notice about the placement of simple sentences in this paragraph? What effect is created through the use and position of these simple sentences?

2 What kind of tone is the writer trying to create? Discuss your ideas in a pair or as a group.

GCSE skills focus

It may help your writing to know that all sentence types have four basic **functions**:

- Statements/declarative sentences – tell you something
- Questions/interrogative sentences – seek an answer to something
- Commands/imperative sentences – give instructions or orders
- Exclamations/exclamatory sentences – are abrupt or excited cries or utterances.

Choosing the right type of sentence for the right job is one way of crafting your writing for effect. Think about the tone, mood or atmosphere you are trying to create. For example, a first-person monologue where the character is unsure and nervous might use lots of little questions to show the character's anxiety.

Now you try it

Write your own paragraph describing a busy place: for example, a beach in summer, a children's play park or the outside of a football ground before a big match.

Try to create and maintain a narrative voice. Perhaps contrast your narrative voice with the mood of the people you are describing – you could describe happy, expectant football fans from the point of view of someone who sees football as pointless. Remember: 'show, don't tell'.

Think about using

- simple sentences to quickly set the time, place and mood
- compound sentences to widen the focus of your description
- complex sentences to enable you to develop your description in detail – try to include some imagery
- a simple sentence to emphasise a particular person, perhaps somebody who looks or behaves differently to the majority.

Top tip

All good writers, not just poets, use imagery (similes, metaphors and **personification**) to add detail and extra depth to their writing.

Key terms

Personification Giving human characteristics to inanimate objects or animals.

Taking it further

Read the following extract from the story 'The Whole Town's Sleeping' by Ray Bradbury.

The central character is rushing to get home, believing she is being followed through a deserted area by a mysterious attacker who has been terrorising her town.

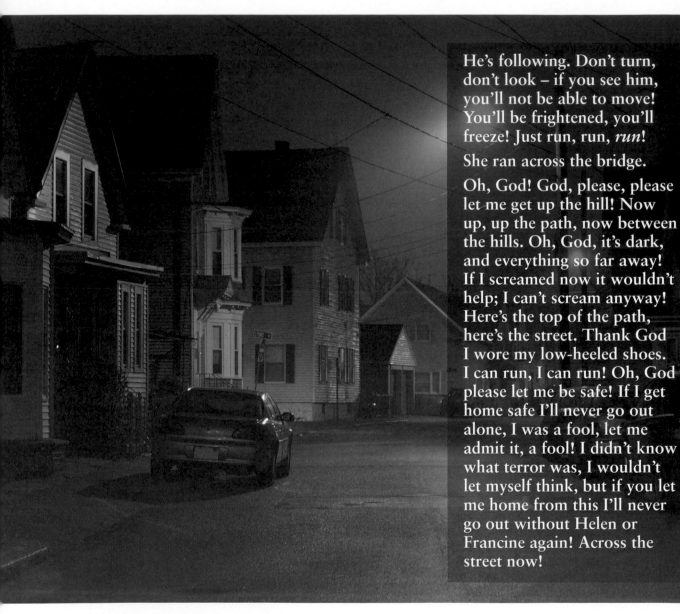

He's following. Don't turn, don't look – if you see him, you'll not be able to move! You'll be frightened, you'll freeze! Just run, run, *run*!

She ran across the bridge.

Oh, God! God, please, please let me get up the hill! Now up, up the path, now between the hills. Oh, God, it's dark, and everything so far away! If I screamed now it wouldn't help; I can't scream anyway! Here's the top of the path, here's the street. Thank God I wore my low-heeled shoes. I can run, I can run! Oh, God please let me be safe! If I get home safe I'll never go out alone, I was a fool, let me admit it, a fool! I didn't know what terror was, I wouldn't let myself think, but if you let me home from this I'll never go out without Helen or Francine again! Across the street now!

1 How has the writer used a variety of sentence structures and punctuation to create a sense of panic? Discuss your ideas with a partner or with your group.

2 Read the extract aloud – either in a pair or in a group. Stop at the end of each sentence and pass the reading to the next person.

Try to emphasise the exclamation marks. Remember, these are there to show heightened emotion. Make your voice sound excited or frightened or relieved.

What did the passage sound like when read aloud? What was the effect of all the short sentences?

3 Notice how Bradbury interrupts the present tense monologue with the short past tense statement: 'She ran across the bridge'. What do you think the effect of this technique is?

4 Working with a partner, write your own short piece of creative writing which deliberately uses a range and variety of sentences to create a sense of panic and tension. Try to spend no more than 15 minutes on this activity.

You may want to include

- some sentence variety
- different sentence types – commands and questions
- repetition of words and phrases for effect
- a range of different punctuation.

Top tip

Whenever you are reading, try to notice how writers manipulate sentences to achieve specific effects.

What have you learnt?

1 Swap your work with another pair. Read their work aloud in your pair, passing the sentences between you as you did with the Bradbury extract.

Is it just as varied? Has this piece of work used short sentences for effect?

Give them some feedback – what did they do well and what would make the writing even better?

2 Take your own feedback and rewrite your work. See if you can make some improvements to make it even more varied and interesting.

Bridge to GCSE

Skilful writers consciously choose which type of sentence they want to use to fulfil a particular purpose. You will be awarded marks for this at GCSE.

Check your level

LEVEL 5 I can use a variety of simple and complex sentences to build up detail.

LEVEL 6 I can compose and shape my sentences deliberately and purposefully.

LEVEL 7 I can control and craft my sentences precisely to suit the overall purpose of my writing.

Learning objective

● To look at effective planning techniques.

Bridge to GCSE

● At GCSE you will need to demonstrate your knowledge, skills and understanding under formal assessed conditions.

One of your GCSE controlled assessments will be a piece of creative writing.

You will be given a task, or a choice of tasks, and you will have the opportunity to plan and prepare before the assessment. You can bring a one-page plan into the assessment, but your final piece will be completed under controlled conditions in a set period of time.

Your task

Here are two examples of the type of task you might be given for a GCSE creative writing controlled assessment.

Task One

The magazine *Thriller Monthly* has launched a writing competition for creative writing enthusiasts. They want the first chapter of a mystery story, submitted in around 600 words.

Task Two

A third-person piece of narrative writing where a character is placed in danger.

GCSE skills focus

Before you can start planning, you need to come up with some ideas of what you're going to write about. Of course, content is very important, but at GCSE there are always more marks awarded for **how** you communicate your ideas rather than **what** your ideas are. So don't spend too long agonising over the subject matter.

Here are two plans for a mystery story called 'The Watcher'. Which one do you think is the most successful, and why?

Plan A

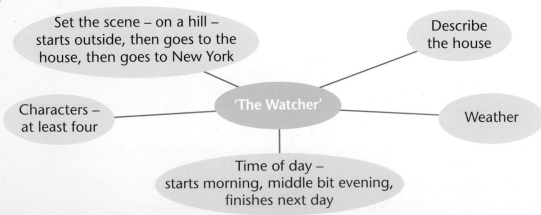

Set the scene – on a hill – starts outside, then goes to the house, then goes to New York

Describe the house

Characters – at least four

'The Watcher'

Weather

Time of day – starts morning, middle bit evening, finishes next day

Plan B

Set the scene gradually – focus on window-pane before panning out

Keep 'watcher' out of first paragraph to add tension

Final sentence – page-turner 'It was time.'

'The Watcher'

Mood – what is the weather like?

Adverbs to suggest emotions ('shifted nervously', 'glanced at watch and frowned...')

One figure – clothing (dark, links to mood), detail (tattooed perhaps, to suggest something from past?)

Use short sentences to emphasise key details and build tension ('What was that?' 'Drip...drip...drip...')

Plan and write your response

1 Now create your own plan for Task One or Task Two. You could write a section of 'The Watcher' for either task.

Aim to make use of all the skills and ideas in this chapter.

Create a spider diagram, or use a table like the one below to draw together all your thoughts and ideas. Add as much detail as you can, and keep adding to it as you come up with new ideas.

Bridge to GCSE

To be successful, focus on small details and develop these well. One well-crafted character is far better than many vague characters.

	What (content)	How (skills)
Setting		
Character/s		
Time of day		
Weather		
Atmosphere		
Events		
Ending		

Bridge to GCSE

For the creative writing task at GCSE you may not use a dictionary or thesaurus. Use your plan to make a note of any key vocabulary, especially if you think you may forget it.

2 Now write the assessed piece of work, referring to your plan.

Checklist for success

✔ Establish setting and introduce characters.
✔ Create appropriate mood and atmosphere.
✔ Show, don't tell.
✔ For effect, use varied sentence structures and suitable words.
✔ Come up with a 'hook' to pull in the reader.

6 Reading and reflecting

Learning objective

- To evaluate your strengths.
- To identify areas for development.

Bridge to GCSE

- At GCSE you will need to develop independence and be able to reflect on how to improve the quality of your own work.

Looking at how other students have approached a task is often one of the most useful ways of making improvements to your own work. For some reason it is much easier to identify the strengths and areas for development in work that is not your own.

You are going to consider two examples of work. Both students have done the same task as you. An examiner has written some comments on the first piece of work. Try reading the example first without reading the comments. Then come up with your own list of strengths and areas for development before seeing what the examiner has to say.

Dean's story

The watcher pointed her binoculars at the empty house; she smiled slightly. The lenses focused on the front door. There was a rusty number 13, a knocker and a slot for mail. There were two newspapers in the mail slot. The lenses then moved around the front of the house, focusing on each of the four dusty windows one by one. One of the panes was broken in the downstairs right window. The watcher pointed the binoculars at the hole and zoomed in to take a closer look. Through the hole, she could see a dusty living room. The television screen was cracked and the coffee table was littered with letters and newspapers. Then the watcher noticed something important. There was a book, it looked like a diary, it had a dragon symbol on the front. The watcher pulled back her glove to reveal a tattoo on her wrist. It was the same dragon symbol!

Examiner comment:

AF1 Dean has maintained the past tense and third person throughout, which helps to establish a clear viewpoint and shows some control of the narrative. Some of the descriptions are developed in detail to add interest; for example, the coffee table. Perhaps Dean could have described the dragon symbol more precisely.

AF3 The paragraph is well structured. It begins with the watcher but does not reveal too much, which keeps the reader interested. The paragraph builds nicely to the cliffhanger of the dragon symbol.

AF5 Dean uses a range of sentences and is usually accurate. Some simple sentences are used for emphasis and Dean is beginning to use complex sentences accurately (for example, 'The lenses then moved…') but does not always get it right and sometimes uses commas where he should use full stops.

Top tip

Using commas rather than full stops is called 'comma splicing' – can you find any other examples in Dean's or David's stories?

AF7 There is some ambitious vocabulary; for example, 'cracked' and 'littered'. However, Dan repeats 'slot', 'pointed' and 'dusty' and could have found more interesting alternatives.

Overall, this is a secure Level 5.

● Set Dean three targets to help him achieve Level 6, using the checklist on page 26.

David's story

A pair of bright, blue, intelligent eyes settled behind the binoculars. Gloved hands adjusted the focusing wheel precisely. A house came into view, isolated and lonely, a small grey smudge on the green valley floor. The blue eyes took in the blood-red roses which grew wild in the untended garden then followed the weed-strewn gravel driveway to the front door. Black paint, cracked and peeling, covered the surface unevenly revealing the rotten wood beneath. Next to the door a small sign bore the name 'Rose Cottage', hinting at a happier past. Whatever secrets the cottage held would be difficult to unravel and the watcher was sure she would not be the only one to try. These thoughts became all too real as two tiny bright circles of light reflected the bright sun from the other side of the valley. Another pair of binoculars, another watcher.

● Imagine you are the examiner. Write a comment for David.
  Try to make a specific point for each AF and give David a Level.

Check your progress

In this chapter, you have been considering how to make your writing interesting to read by deliberately crafting your language. You've planned and written an effective story opening, thinking about how to engage the reader with your vocabulary and sentence structure, and by withholding information.

Taking it further

Which Level do you think you have reached in this chapter, and what do you need to do to improve?

LEVEL 5 (Aiming for GCSE C/B)

AF1 I can use some imaginative details to make my writing interesting.

AF3 I can deliberately organise my sentences and paragraphs to create a sense of mystery and tension.

AF5 I can choose the right type of sentence for the right purpose.

AF7 I can use particular words to add to the tone and atmosphere.

LEVEL 6 (Aiming for GCSE B/A)

AF1 I can develop some really interesting details.

AF3 I can deliberately use the opening of a piece of writing to engage the reader.

AF5 I can control the way I use simple and complex sentences to achieve the right tone and atmosphere.

AF7 I can choose the right words to add to the tone and atmosphere now that I am developing a wider vocabulary.

LEVEL 7 (Aiming for GCSE A/A*)

AF1 I can successfully produce a piece of imaginative atmospheric writing.

AF3 I can deliberately shape the writing, including the opening, to completely engage and sustain the reader's interest.

AF5 I can manipulate my sentences deliberately to achieve the effect I want to create.

AF7 I can match the wide vocabulary I use to my purpose and the tone I want to create.

Next steps to GCSE

For GCSE, you will have to sustain your learning by planning and writing some longer pieces of creative work under controlled conditions. You will have to adapt your writing to suit a range of audiences and purposes, controlling your vocabulary, sentence structure and paragraphing as well as your content and ideas.

Chapter 2

Reading creative texts

In this chapter you will look at how writers create characters in novels and short stories. You will explore how stories are told, and how we are made to feel about characters and narrators. You will start to think about how writers use language, structure and form to introduce ideas to the reader.

Bridge to GCSE

To get you ready for your GCSE course, this chapter will take you through the following steps:

Explore ideas
- Understand language, structure and narrative perspective.
- Analyse and use evidence from the text like a GCSE student.

Check your skills
- Write about how writers create character.

Extend your skills
- Analyse the effects of unusual narrative perspectives.

Plan and write
- Plan a piece of analytical writing and create a 'notes page'.
- Write effectively under timed conditions.

Improve your work
- Review your response and set yourself a target for improvement.

Your GCSE-style assessment task will be a timed analysis of a prose fiction extract.

Key Stage 3 Reading Assessment Focuses	GCSE English/English Language Assessment Objectives
AF3 Deduce, infer or interpret information, events or ideas from texts	**AO2/3i** Read and understand texts, selecting material appropriate to purpose […]
AF5 Explain and comment on writers' use of language, including grammatical and literary features at word and sentence level	**AO2/3ii** Develop and sustain interpretations of writers' ideas and perspectives
AF6 Identify and comment on writers' purposes and viewpoints, and the overall effect of the text on the reader	**AO2/3iii** Explain and evaluate how writers use linguistic, grammatical, structural and presentational features to achieve effects and engage and influence the reader

Characterisation

Learning objective
- To explore how a writer creates an overall impression of a character.

Bridge to GCSE
- At GCSE you will need to consider the choices writers make when writing a creative text.

Writers make deliberate choices about how to present their characters, choices that shape our responses to these characters.

When exploring character at GCSE, you will need to think about the writer's choice of
- language (words, images, sentences)
- structure (what we are shown first, what is revealed when)
- form (in a novel, who is telling the story and from what viewpoint).

Getting you thinking

Read the opening paragraphs of the first chapter of *Great Expectations* by Charles Dickens.

The novel is narrated in the **first person** by the adult Pip. He begins the story with an early childhood memory – being alone as a small boy in a graveyard, surrounded by the gravestones of his dead family.

Key terms

First person The narrator is part of the story, which is told from their point of view. Uses 'I'.

My father's family name being Pirrip, and my Christian name Philip, my infant tongue could make of both names nothing longer or more explicit than Pip. So, I called myself Pip, and came to be called Pip.

I give Pirrip as my father's family name, on the authority of his tombstone and my sister – Mrs Joe Gargery, who married the blacksmith. As I never saw my father or my mother, and never saw any likeness of either of them (for their days were long before the days of photographs), my first fancies regarding what they were like, were unreasonably derived from their tombstones. The shape of the letters on my father's, gave me an odd idea that he was a square, stout, dark man, with curly black hair. From the character and turn of the inscription, *Also Georgiana Wife of the Above*, I drew a childish conclusion that my mother was freckled and sickly. To five little stone lozenges, each about a foot and a half long, which were arranged in a neat row beside their grave, and were sacred to the memory of five little brothers of mine – who gave up trying to get a living exceedingly early in that universal struggle – I am indebted for a belief I religiously entertained that they had all been born on their backs with their hands in their trousers-pockets, and had never taken them out in this state of existence.

Ours was the marsh country, down by the river, within, as the river wound, twenty miles of the sea. My first most vivid and broad impression of the identity of things, seems to me to have been gained on a memorable raw afternoon towards evening. At such a time I found out for certain, that this bleak place overgrown with nettles was the churchyard; and that Philip Pirrip, late of this parish, and also Georgiana wife of the above, were dead and buried; and that Alexander, Bartholomew, Abraham, Tobias, and Roger, infant children of the aforesaid, were also dead and buried; and that the dark flat wilderness beyond the churchyard, intersected with dykes and mounds and gates, with scattered cattle feeding on it, was the marshes; and that the low leaden line beyond was the river; and that the distant savage lair from which the wind was rushing, was the sea; and that the small bundle of shivers growing afraid of it all and beginning to cry, was Pip.

1 What impression of Pip's feelings and situation does Dickens create here? Read the extract carefully a couple of times and note down some ideas about

- how you think Pip is feeling
- how you think Dickens wants you to feel about Pip.

GCSE skills focus

You may have decided that Dickens wants the reader to feel sympathy for the young Pip. What might have led you to that conclusion?

You should read like a detective:

- Focus on details and make deductions from them.
- Always be prepared to prove your points with evidence and/or quotations from the text. A good lawyer always has evidence for his or her statements – a good English student should have the same.

Now you try it

Finding relevant, appropriate evidence is a very important skill. Your evidence can be an actual quotation, a reference to something that happens to one of the characters or information about the setting.

1 Find some evidence to support the following points about why we sympathise with Pip. Make sure each piece of evidence strongly proves the point, but keep quotations short (they don't have to be full sentences). Two points have been supported with evidence for you – the first uses a quotation and the second gives some information about the setting.

Point	Evidence
Pip is small.	'small bundle of shivers'
Pip is alone.	He is surrounded by the graves of his family and he doesn't mention anybody else being with him.
Pip is an orphan.	
Pip feels cold.	
Pip misses his parents.	
Pip is in a frightening place.	
Pip seems sad and afraid.	
Pip appears to be very lonely and vulnerable.	

Taking it further

Now that you have made some points and found evidence to back them up, you can begin to apply what you have discovered.

Think about this question:

How does Dickens give the reader a first impression of Pip?

When writing about literary texts, it is useful to follow the structure Point – Evidence – Explanation (P-E-E). You should aim to:

● make a clear **P**oint

  Pip appears to be very lonely and vulnerable.

● support with **E**vidence

  He is described as a 'small bundle of shivers growing afraid of it all'.

- **E**xplain using a developed, detailed account of how this makes you feel towards Pip, bringing in more evidence. This is the most important element and should always be the longest and most detailed.

> This suggests that Pip is isolated and all on his own. The word 'shivers', makes him sound cold as well as frightened as the word suggests two meanings. The word 'small' also stresses how little and young Pip is at this point in the book, which engages the reader's sympathy and makes us feel worried about him being alone in the 'dark flat wilderness'.

Comments on the effects of particular words

Analyses the effects of particular word choices on the reader

1 Using the model above, take one of the points from your table and construct your own paragraph of P-E-E. Make sure that:

- the explanation is detailed and developed
- you have used at least one additional piece of evidence in your explanation.

2 Why do you think Dickens chose to open his novel in this way? With a partner, discuss and write down your thoughts about the following ideas:

a Why might Dickens have started by describing his character when he was a small child and unable to pronounce his own name? What is the effect of this piece of information?

b What is the effect of the choice of name – 'Pip'? What other meanings might this word have? What might Dickens be suggesting about the character by this choice of name?

> **Bridge to GCSE**
>
> Start to question and explore Dickens's use of language. GCSE readers focus on writers' techniques and purposes rather than just the 'story'.

What have you learnt?

Choose five interesting words from the opening section of *Great Expectations*.

Explain to a partner why you chose each of these words. See if you can talk for at least a minute about one of the words, explaining in detail why it is an interesting choice of word and what effect it has on you and your understanding of Pip.

Check your level

LEVEL 5 I can find relevant evidence to show how a writer has used language for effect.

LEVEL 6 I can comment in some detail on the effects of particular words and phrases.

LEVEL 7 I can analyse how a writer uses language deliberately for effect, starting to look at different interpretations.

Looking at language

Learning objective

- To explore how writers use language to create characters.
- To think about the ways in which language can be used to create different effects on the reader.

Bridge to GCSE

- At GCSE you will be expected to focus on details and analyse effects.

As a GCSE student you will need to think about how writers create impressions on the reader. If you can consider the effects of particular words and language techniques, ask questions of the text and offer different interpretations, then you are *analysing language*.

Analysis is very important to Level 7 and GCSE. As you are reading, ask yourself:

- **What is the writer doing here?**
- **How is the writer getting their ideas across?**

Make links between ideas and consider layers of meaning.

Getting you thinking

1 Look again at the extract from *Great Expectations* on pages 28–29. Working with a partner, see if you can identify all of the language choices in the third paragraph that create a gloomy, negative impression of the setting.

As well as a writer's choice of words, 'language' can also mean:

- **imagery** such as metaphors and similes
- **patterns** such as alliteration and repetition
- **perspective:** for example, first or third person.

Here is how one student began to analyse the paragraph. The student has highlighted words and phrases in the text and made notes on the effects being created.

> Ours was the marsh country, down by the river, within, as the river wound, twenty miles of the sea. My first most vivid and broad impression of the identity of things, seems to me to have been gained on a memorable raw afternoon towards evening. At such a time I found out for certain, that this bleak place overgrown with nettles was the churchyard; and that Philip Pirrip, late of this parish, and also Georgiana wife of the above, were dead and buried; and that Alexander, Bartholomew, Abraham, Tobias, and Roger, infant children of the aforesaid, were also dead and buried; and that the dark flat wilderness beyond the churchyard, intersected with dykes and mounds and gates, with scattered cattle feeding on it, was the marshes; and that the low leaden line beyond, was the river; and that the distant savage lair from which the wind was rushing, was the sea; and that the small bundle of shivers growing afraid of it all and beginning to cry, was Pip.

The student's notes are moving towards Level 7 in the way they explore and begin to analyse the effects of particular language choices, asking questions, suggesting different interpretations or commenting on effects.

Ours ... marsh country: Will be flat and empty as much of the area will be waterlogged.

Raw: suggests so cold that it is painful.

Evening: suggests that it is getting dark, therefore more threatening.

Bleak: 'Bleak' sounds gloomy and miserable as well as empty and lonely. It almost sounds hopeless.

Overgrown with nettles: Nettles are a weed – if the graveyard is 'overgrown' with nettles then it is probably isolated and uncared for. Nettles can also inflict pain. Could this link to Pip somehow?

GCSE skills focus

Analytical readers look for different interpretations and layers of meaning. They also make links between ideas.

To begin to analyse as well as explain language effects, try replacing 'this shows that' with some of these terms instead:

- This highlights…
- This suggests…
- This implies…
- This demonstrates…
- Alternatively…

Now you try it

1 Look at the notes the student has made on page 33. Take each of the six highlighted sections of text that haven't yet had been analysed and write some notes of your own. Focus on the effects of

- repetition
- word choices
- imagery (similes, metaphors)
- alliteration
- use of third person.

2 Now take one phrase and see how much you can say about it. Here is an example:

Sounds unfamiliar to him, as if he has never been before and doesn't know what it is called

A gloomy, miserable word

'this bleak place overgrown with nettles'

A weed – suggests lack of care, again linking to Pip. Also hints at pain and danger, as if foreshadowing what is to come later.

Suggests that it is not looked after, which suggests that there is nobody else there and that creates the idea that Pip is very isolated and unprotected. It could also imply that he is not looked after.

3 Working with a partner, choose another of the highlighted phrases. Write it on a sheet of plain paper. Write down as much as you can about the feelings or ideas being suggested by your phrase. Don't spend too long doing this; your initial thoughts are often the most insightful.

4 Swap your paper with another pair (make sure they have chosen a different phrase). Take another five minutes to see how much you can add to the ideas they have had about their phrase.

5 Share your ideas with the class. How many different ideas did you all manage to come up with about one phrase?

> **Bridge to GCSE**
>
> This is 'lot about a little' analysis. You have examined the writer's choice of a few specific words in considerable depth. Developing this kind of skill is fantastic preparation for GCSE, as you will gain more marks for analysing a few things in detail than trying to write about lots of different points.

Taking it further

Use the student's notes (and your own) to write your own analysis of Dickens's use of language in this passage. You are focusing on this question:

How does Dickens use language to influence the reader's response to Pip?

You can use P-E-E as your model. Remember to include some analysis phrases such as the ones on page 33 rather than 'this shows that'. Aim to write at least 200 words.

You could start like this:

> Dickens uses the setting of an isolated graveyard to present Pip as vulnerable and lonely, perhaps implying that he is completely abandoned and at the mercy of the world around him...

★ Top tip

You must use evidence to support the points you are making. Look back at pages 28–31 for a reminder if you need to.

What have you learnt?

Look at this checklist and consider what progress you are making with your GCSE reading skills. Then read a partner's work and offer a comment or target based on the list.

Bridge to GCSE

One way of staying focused on the writer's purpose and techniques is to use their last name whenever you can. Try starting sentences with 'Dickens creates...', 'Dickens is highlighting...' and so on.

Checklist for success

✔ Focus on the effects of particular words and phrases.

✔ Mention the writer's name and use phrases like 'Dickens (or the writer) is suggesting/highlighting/implying...'

✔ Use plenty of short, relevant evidence in your writing.

✔ Use some analysis vocabulary rather than 'this shows that...'.

✔ Start to consider deeper, hidden layers of meaning that are suggested by the way the author tells the story.

✔ Rather than making one straightforward comment develop and explain ideas in detail.

Check your level

LEVEL 5 I can comment on the effects of particular words and phrases.

LEVEL 6 I can explain effects of particular words and phrases in quite a lot of detail.

LEVEL 7 I can provide in-depth analysis of effects of a particular word or phrase.

Learning objective

- To explore the ways writers use structure and form to present their characters.

Bridge to GCSE

- At GCSE you will need to consider how writers structure and organise their material.

Writers don't just throw their ideas at the page in any random order. Deciding what to tell the reader when, and how, is all part of the *structure*. The writer will have consciously decided what the reader sees first, who is introduced first, and why.

The writer will also have deliberately decided who is telling the story – whose *narrative perspective* to use. This is all part of *form*. Being able to comment on the *structure* and *form* of the text is an essential skill for GCSE.

Getting you thinking

Reread the first two paragraphs from *Great Expectations* on pages 28–29.

Key terms

Narrative perspective The point of view of the person telling the story.

1 Why does Dickens focus on Pip right at the start of the novel? What does that tell the reader about the story to come? Share your ideas with the class.

2 Dickens has chosen a first-person narrative perspective. How does this point of view affect the reader's response?

3 Study the last sentence in the second paragraph. Think about the effect of the structure of this sentence.

Here's what one student had to say.

> Dickens's use of sentence structure in this passage conveys that Pip is gradually becoming more and more aware of the surrounding environment and growing more and more afraid as a result. The long sentence builds up to the final phrase 'was Pip' as if to highlight his loneliness and isolation.

GCSE skills focus

Reading for 'layers of meaning' is a very important skill to develop if you want to progress beyond Level 6. Good writers will often **imply** ideas through small details – they will 'show, not tell'. One particular detail, or word choice, or sentence, or position in the story, can be used to **imply** an idea to the reader.

Sometimes writers hide an **implied** meaning underneath a **surface** (or literal meaning). You are going to consider how Dickens does this in the next extract from *Great Expectations*.

Now you try it

Read the fourth paragraph of *Great Expectations*, which introduces the character of Magwitch, a convict.

> 'Hold your noise!' cried a terrible voice, as a man started up from among the graves at the side of the church porch. 'Keep still, you little devil, or I'll cut your throat!'
>
> A fearful man, all in coarse grey, with a great iron on his leg. A man with no hat, and with broken shoes, and with an old rag tied round his head. A man who had been soaked in water, and smothered in mud, and lamed by stones, and cut by flints, and stung by nettles, and torn by briars; who limped, and shivered, and glared and growled; and whose teeth chattered in his head as he seized me by the chin.

1 How do you think Dickens wants the reader to react to Magwitch?

2 Working with a partner, copy out the words and phrases that make Magwitch sound dangerous and threatening.

There are several ways in which Dickens gives the reader a strong first impression of Magwitch and the effect he has on Pip.

3 Make the following bullet points into a paragraph of writing about the effect of Magwitch's entrance on Pip. You will need to find some supporting evidence to prove what you say. Remember, **P**oint – **E**vidence – **E**xplanation.

- He makes a sudden, dramatic entrance.
- His first words to Pip are commanding and threatening.
- His appearance is unusual in several ways.
- He has 'an iron' on his leg.
- He is physically violent to Pip.

4 However, things aren't as straightforward as they might have appeared. We need to start considering 'layers of meaning'.

Working again in pairs, write, in another colour, the words and phrases that make Magwitch seem vulnerable and weak.

Let's look at one student's analysis of this section of the text.

Point =   Magwitch has escaped from prison

Evidence =   'all in coarse grey with a great iron on his leg'

Explanation =   In a few words Dickens shows that Magwitch is wearing some kind of uniform made of cheap fabric and a leg iron.

Point =   Magwitch's appearance was unusual and shabby. Starting to suggest desperation and poverty – vulnerability.

Evidence =   'A man with no hat', 'broken shoes' and ' old rag tied round his head'

Explanation =   At the time of the book all men wore hats outside, it would have been very unusual not to have one on, the rag is rather a pathetic way to keep his head covered.

Point =   Appears to be very weak

Evidence =   'soaked in water...lamed by stones'

Explanation =   Dickens's use of verbs suggests that Magwitch is under attack here – as though he is being beaten down by the environment. Rather than making him seem threatening, he appears vulnerable and weak and in pain, as hinted by painful verbs like 'stung' and 'cut'.

Point =   Shows signs of physical weakness

Evidence =   'limped, and shivered'

Explanation =   We find out Magwitch is injured and cold. Could 'shivered' also link to fear, perhaps? Compare with 'little bundle of shivers'.

Point =   Magwitch is scared

Evidence =   'teeth chattered in his head'

Explanation =   Implies fear as well as being cold and wet.

So although on the surface Magwitch appears to be dangerous and threatening, Dickens implies that he is also weak and vulnerable.

Taking it further

Did you notice the similarity between Dickens's use of long sentences with lots of clauses for both the description of Pip and the description of Magwitch? Do you think this is deliberate?

● Why do you think the introduction of these two characters might have been **juxtaposed** in this way? Discuss with a partner.

> **Key terms**
>
> **Juxtaposed** Two ideas placed next to each other for deliberate, contrasting effect.

> **Bridge to GCSE**
>
> Consider *why* Dickens uses the same sentence structure for both characters – possibly to suggest a link, connection or similarity between them?

What have you learnt?

Now that you can identify the ways Dickens has presented **layers of meaning** through **structure** and **form**, it's time to demonstrate your understanding with a piece of writing.

Answer the following question:

How does Dickens use structure and form to present characters to the reader in the opening of Great Expectations?

Checklist for success

✓ Write about 250–300 words.

✓ Provide useful, short and relevant pieces of evidence.

✓ Use analysis vocabulary rather than 'this shows that…'.

✓ Use the writer's name: 'Dickens does this' or 'Dickens presents'.

✓ Refer to how the young Pip might be affected by Magwitch's appearance and behaviour.

✓ Compare the presentation of Pip and the presentation of Magwitch.

✓ Make a comment on why the two characters are introduced side by side.

Check your level	**LEVEL 5**	I can describe some structure choices made by the writer.
	LEVEL 6	I can start to explore how the writer has used structure to shape the reader's responses..
	LEVEL 7	I can evaluate the ways the writer has made structure and form choices to create meaning.

Learning objective

- To develop your ability to select relevant and appropriate evidence.
- To learn how to comment effectively on how the writer uses language.

Bridge to GCSE

- At GCSE using well-chosen evidence is a powerful way of improving your grade.

How often have you made a judgement about somebody you have met based on what they are wearing, or something they say, or something that they do?

Writers use subtle signals to communicate their ideas about their characters to the reader. Good writers *imply* meaning – they ask the reader to 'read between the lines', making deductions from the hints they are giving us. Our job as readers is to *infer* meaning. As in real life, a good reader sees a character and works out what they are like from the clues the writer gives them.

Getting you thinking

The following extract is from the novel *The Silence of the Lambs* by Thomas Harris. A doctor is warning a young FBI agent how to behave when she questions a very dangerous murderer.

Then you should be able to remember the rules: Do not reach through the bars, do not touch the bars. You pass him nothing but soft paper. No pens, no pencils. He has his own felt-tipped pens some of the time. The paper you pass him must be free of staples, paper clips, or pins. Items come back out through the sliding food carrier. No exceptions. Do not accept anything he attempts to hold out to you through the barrier. Do you understand me?

1 What do you notice about the type of sentences the writer uses here?

2 Think about the content of the commands. Consider the following details:
- 'soft paper'
- 'felt-tipped pens'
- 'No pens, no pencils'
- 'free of staples, paper clips or pins'.

Discuss with a partner what these details suggest about the murderer. What can you infer about him?

3 Now think about the sentence: 'Do not reach through the bars, do not touch the bars.' Where else might you come across a warning like this?

Write a paragraph explaining what the writer is implying about the murderer from the command sentences used here.

 Top tip

Focusing on why a writer has done something and its effect will raise your Level.

GCSE skills focus

Inference is a really important skill. It means you are picking up the signals the writer is sending. It also means you are starting to consider 'layers of meaning'.

Once you have drawn the inferences from the text, you need to demonstrate your reading skills by writing down your ideas. It is important to know how to do this effectively as it is the main way you are assessed at GCSE. You need to support your points with evidence from the text.

Embedded quotations are short words or phrases from the text that you insert into your own sentences. Look at the difference between the following two pieces of work.

Student A

The criminal sounds very dangerous:

'The paper you pass him must be free of staples, paper clips, or pins'.

This shows that he is dangerous because he is not allowed to be given anything sharp, even though it is something small and quite innocent like a paper clip.

Student B

The writer suggests that this man is very dangerous through the long list of instructions the doctor gives Starling. Even the innocent paper 'must be free of staples, paper clips and pins', which implies that not only is he dangerous but also very intelligent as he can presumably turn an innocent 'paper clip' into some form of weapon or means of escape.

Notice how student B's paragraph flows much better than student A's. Although both are following P-E-E, student B has 'embedded' short pieces of evidence skilfully into his or her own sentences.

Now you try it

Read this extract from 'The Speckled Band' by Sir Arthur Conan Doyle. Dr Watson describes the arrival of Sir Grimesby Roylott at Sherlock Holmes's rooms in 221b Baker Street. Holmes discovers that …

> … our door had been suddenly dashed open, and that a huge man had framed himself in the **aperture**. His costume was a peculiar mixture of the professional and of the agricultural, having a black top-hat, a long frock-coat, and a pair of high gaiters, with a **hunting-crop** swinging in his hand. So tall was he that his hat actually brushed the cross bar of the-doorway, and his breadth seemed to span it across from side to side. A large face, seared with a thousand wrinkles, burned yellow with the sun, and marked with every evil passion, was turned from one to the other of us, while his deep-set, **bile**-shot eyes, and his high, thin, fleshless nose, gave him somewhat the **resemblance** to a fierce old bird of prey.

Sir Grimesby Roylott is a very unpleasant, dangerous character. You are going to write a paragraph analysing how Conan Doyle reveals this to the reader.

1 Working with a partner, first of all read this extract closely a few times. You might want to read it out loud to each other.

2 Next, choose five pieces of evidence that you want to use in your writing. Some of the most interesting ones have been highlighted for you already.

3 What does each one suggest about Sir Grimesby Roylott? What can you infer?

📖 Glossary

Always have a dictionary to hand, to look up any unfamiliar words. In 'The Speckled Band' extract, the following definitions might be useful:

Aperture Hole or opening which lets light through.

Hunting-crop Short whip without a lash.

Bile Bitter-tasting liquid.

Resemblance Looking like.

Bridge to GCSE

Candidates aiming for Grade C at GCSE need to be able to offer relevant and appropriate quotations to support the points they make.

Here is an example of how one student has written the first part of their paragraph:

Conan Doyle presents Sir Grimesby Roylott as a very unpleasant, dangerous character. His arrival makes the reader jump as well as Holmes and Watson, because the door is 'suddenly dashed open' which makes it sound quite violent and shocking. Also he is described as 'huge' and 'tall' and he takes up the whole doorway. This is threatening because it implies he is very physically powerful. It also suggests that he is blocking the escape route for Holmes and Watson...

Clear focus on the task

Comments on the effects of a particular word with an embedded quotation

The word 'also' shows that they are developing their ideas

The student is looking at alternative ideas and suggestions

Taking it further

Using the evidence you have collected, answer this question:

How does Conan Doyle present Sir Grimesby Roylott as an unpleasant, dangerous character?

Checklist for success

✔ Show that you are focused clearly on the task.

✔ Comment on the effects of particular words and phrases.

✔ Use evidence in the form of embedded quotations.

✔ Use the word 'also' to develop some alternative ideas.

✔ Try to write about 200 words.

 Bridge to GCSE

Look for alternatives to the following overused phrases:

'I know this because…'

'This shows that…'

Check your level

LEVEL 4 I can generally identify the right quotation to use.

LEVEL 5 I can identify the right quotation to use to support my comments on language effects.

LEVEL 6 I can use short, effective embedded quotations to make my writing flow.

Learning objective
- To analyse how writers use narrative perspective to create different effects.

Bridge to GCSE
- At GCSE you will consider writers' choices of narrative perspective and analyse the effects on the reader.

Using first-person narrative perspective builds a relationship between the reader and the main character and encourages readers to care about what happens to the character – a very good reason to keep reading a story. However, sometimes the narrator is not someone we should trust.

Getting you thinking

Look at the opening paragraph of 'The Tell-Tale Heart' by Edgar Allan Poe.

It is a first-person narrative – we never find out the name of the narrator, nor where he is as he tells the story. Poe reveals details gradually to build tension and suspense.

Discuss the following questions either with a partner or in a group:

- Do we assume that because we are in a narrator's ' head' we will be getting the truth?
- Does seeing things from the narrator's point of view mean we tend to be on their side?
- In 'The Tell-Tale Heart', do we assume that this narrator is telling the truth?
- Why might people be calling him 'mad'?

TRUE! – nervous – very, very dreadfully nervous I had been and am; but why *will* you say that I am mad? The disease had sharpened my senses, not destroyed – not dulled them. Above all was the sense of hearing acute. I heard all things in the heaven and in the earth. I heard many things in hell. How then am I mad? Hearken! and observe how healthily – how calmly, I can tell you the whole story.

GCSE skills focus

Unpleasant characters usually provide some kind of challenge to the main character(s). This builds tension and encourages us to care more about the main character(s). For example, Dickens makes us dislike Magwitch for how he makes Pip feel in Chapter One of *Great Expectations* and this only encourages us to sympathise with Pip even further.

However, sometimes writers will use an unpleasant, **unsympathetic** main character to make a deliberate point.

Now you try it

If we look more closely at 'The Tell-Tale Heart', it starts to become clear that the narrator might not be telling the truth and that the people who have called him 'mad' are right.

Poe has created an **unreliable narrator**. This means that there is often a gap (ironic distance) between what the narrator tells us and what has actually happened. This makes the story engaging because, as we read, we have to constantly check what the narrator is telling us and **infer meaning** to get at the truth.

> **Key terms**
>
> **Unreliable narrator** The person narrating the story is someone not to be trusted for some reason.

1 Copy out and complete the table below. How does each piece of evidence hint that we are not to trust this narrator's account of events?

Evidence	Comment
The narrator's speech is broken and disjointed with lots of exclamations and words in capitals.	
'The disease had sharpened my senses'	
'I heard all things in the heaven and in the earth.'	
'I heard many things in hell.'	
'…observe how healthily, how calmly, I can tell you the whole story.'	

2 Read the rest of the story for yourself. Either use the copy from the *A Bridge to GCSE Teacher Guide* or follow the link below:

www.literature.org/authors/poe-edgar-allan/tell-tale-heart.html

3 Answer this question: *How does Poe use the technique of unreliable narration to create tension and engage the interest of the reader in 'The Tell-Tale Heart'?*

What have you learnt?

Swap your work with a partner. Mark each other's work using the checklist shown on the right.

Checklist for success

✔ Find examples of how the narrator is unreliable.
✔ Look out for specific techniques; for example, direct questions to the reader, as if he is seeking understanding.
✔ Make detailed comments about the effects of specific words, phrases and sentences.

Check your level

LEVEL 6 I can start to explore some of the ways a writer uses language and structure.

LEVEL 7 I can begin to analyse and evaluate the methods a writer uses to present their ideas and viewpoints.

LEVEL 8 I can evaluate how the language, structure and form of a text supports the writer's purpose.

Learning objective

- To explore how to make a notes page for controlled assessment.

Bridge to GCSE

- At GCSE you will need to make a 'notes page' each time you have a controlled assessment.

You are going to continue your exploration of narrative style and perspective by analysing a new extract.

Your task

You will need a sheet of plain paper. Write down the following GCSE-style assessment task:

> **How does Harper Lee use language, structure and/or form to present the character of Mrs Dubose to the reader in *To Kill a Mockingbird*?**

Read the extract below, from *To Kill a Mockingbird* by Harper Lee. This novel is narrated by Scout, a little girl living in America's Deep South during the depression of the 1930s. In this section we are introduced to Mrs Dubose, one of Scout's neighbours and, in many ways, a deeply unsympathetic character.

When we were small, Jem and I confined our activities to the southern neighbourhood, but when I was well into the second grade at school and tormenting Boo Radley became passé, the business section of Maycomb drew us frequently up the street past the real property of Mrs Henry Lafayette Dubose. It was impossible to go into town without passing her house unless we wished to walk a mile out of the way. Previous minor encounters with her left me with no desire for more, but Jem said I had to grow up some time.

Mrs Dubose lived alone except for a Negro girl in constant attendance, two doors up the street from us in a house with steep front steps and a dog-trot hall. She was very old; she spent most of each day in bed and the rest of it in a wheel-chair. It was rumoured that she kept a C.S.A. pistol concealed among her numerous shawls and wraps.

Jem and I hated her. If she was on the porch when we passed, we would be raked by her wrathful gaze, subjected to ruthless interrogation regarding our behaviour, and given a melancholy prediction on what we would amount to when we grew up, which was always nothing. We had long ago given up the idea of walking past her house on the opposite side of the street; that only made her raise her voice and let the whole neighbourhood in on it.

We could do nothing to please her. If I said as sunnily as I could, 'Hey, Mrs Dubose,' I would receive for an answer, 'Don't you say hey to me, you ugly girl! You say good afternoon, Mrs Dubose!'

GCSE skills focus

Scout portrays Mrs Dubose in a very negative way. Note down the evidence which presents Mrs Dubose as unpleasant.

You might think about some of the following points:

- the way the narrator uses Mrs Dubose's full name
- effects of particular words and phrases (*raked, ruthless, interrogation, melancholy,* and so on)
- use and position of sentences for effect
- her behaviour towards the children
- her use of insults
- rumours about her
- the narrator's feelings – is the reader sympathetic?

Make a note of these analysis vocabulary phrases:

> This could highlight...
> This could possibly suggest...
> Alternatively, this could also imply...
> Perhaps another interpretation could be...

Your notes page should now contain:

- the assessment task
- lots of useful evidence in the form of words and phrases
- helpful analysis vocabulary phrases.

Bridge to GCSE

Avoid using full sentences on your notes page. Use words and phrases only.

Checklist for success

✓ Find and use appropriate, relevant evidence.

✓ Embed your evidence into your sentences.

✓ Develop points in detail using analytical vocabulary.

✓ Consider the point of view of the narrator.

✓ Refer to the writer by her last name.

Plan your response

You have written the title of the assessment task on your notes page, along with the evidence you have selected so far.

Bridge to GCSE

Remember that your teacher/examiner already knows the story. Never retell or describe what happens. You are not being assessed for knowing the story and you will waste time.

1 In another colour or pencil, underline what you think are the key words in the task. Have you chosen the same key words as in the table below? Using the points in the right-hand column, make notes on the extract that will help you in your assessment task.

Key words	Points to focus on
How	Focus on the writer's craft, don't retell the story or explain who the characters are
language	Vocabulary/images/alliteration/repetition etc.
structure	Use of sentence structure for effect, order in which information is revealed
form	Use of child narrator and first-person perspective
unpleasant characters	How the characters are described – what they do/say, how they behave
to the reader	How the reader is supposed to react/feel

Here is how a student has organised some of his ideas:

Lee uses some very negative language to present Mrs Dubose. In the third paragraph, Scout describes how they were 'raked' by Mrs Dubose's 'wrathful gaze'. The word 'raked' not only suggests a detailed scrutiny, but also implies that it was painful in some way – as if her gaze made them feel extremely uncomfortable. 'Wrathful' appears very over the top, possibly implying that Mrs Dubose gets angry very easily and is unreasonable.

— uses writer's name

— focuses on question

— use of evidence, embedded into sentence

— analytical vocabulary

— narrator's point of view

2 Choose any of the points from your notes page.

Allow yourself five minutes to write a paragraph in the style of the notes above. Try to include all the points that have been highlighted in the student's notes.

Write your response

3 You are now ready to start your writing task. Make sure you have your notes page and a clean copy of the extract to hand. Refer to the assessment objectives on page 27 to remind yourself of what gets marks.

Checklist for success

✔ You should allow yourself at least one hour to complete this task.

✔ Aim to write 500–600 words.

✔ Use relevant evidence.

✔ Consider the point of view of the narrator.

✔ Use analytical vocabulary.

✔ Refer to the writer by her name.

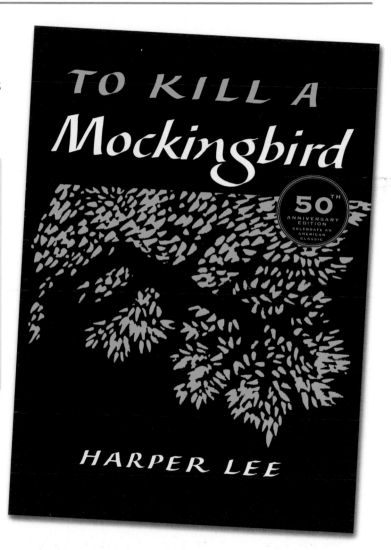

TO KILL A Mockingbird

50TH ANNIVERSARY EDITION CELEBRATE AN AMERICAN CLASSIC

HARPER LEE

Learning objective

- To evaluate your strengths and areas for development.

Bridge to GCSE

- At GCSE it is important to review your own work and make any necessary alterations.

Now you have completed your writing task, it is important to think about what you have learnt through this process, what your achievements have been, and what you need to focus on to make even more progress. This is really useful GCSE preparation as it means you are starting to take some real responsibility for your own learning and development.

Getting you thinking

Read Hannah's response. She was working on the same task as you.

> In this passage the children are scared of Mrs Dubose. You know they are scared because they try to walk on the other side of the road so they don't go past her house. Also the writer says that she has a pistol so they might be scared that she will shoot them. She shouts at them all the time and insults them, like when she says 'don't you say hey to me, you ugly girl!' This makes her sound unkind and also unfair as the girl hasn't done anything wrong and has tried to be friendly. She must say some things that are embarrassing because the girl is worried that the whole neighbourhood will hear. The language used to describe her makes her sound angry and dangerous with words like 'wrathful' and 'ruthless'.

Examiner comment:

AF3 Hannah has inferred meaning several times. The comment 'the children are scared of Mrs Dubose' is rather basic but 'she must say some things that are embarrassing' is better because Hannah is interpreting feelings and ideas from the text. Hannah has used some pieces of the text as relevant quotation to support her points.

AF5 Towards the end of the work Hannah has written a sentence which focuses on language effects – it is quite a straightforward comment but accurate, and shows that Hannah is starting to think about the writer's use of language for effect.

AF6 There is a clear sense that the writer has deliberately done things for effect. Hannah could have made much more of the idea that a child is telling the story, however.

Overall, this is a secure Level 5.

- Using the checklist on page 52, set Hannah three targets to help her achieve Level 6.

GCSE skills focus

The three main areas of focus for GCSE Reading are
- understanding the meanings, ideas and attitudes presented in what you are reading
- being able to explain and engage with writers' ideas, using evidence
- understanding and analysing writers' use of language, structure and form to present ideas.

Now you try it

1 Choose one paragraph of your writing task that you feel was particularly effective and successful.

Swap your paragraph with a partner.

Use the checklist on page 52 to mark the paragraph, highlighting examples from the paragraph which meet the assessment criteria.

2 Choose the most successful extract from the paragraph. It may be a sentence using embedded evidence well, or a good idea explored, or skilful use of analysis vocabulary. Share the extract you have chosen with the class and explain why you chose it.

3 Give your partner a target for improvement. What will move them towards the next level?

Taking it further

Rewrite your chosen paragraph to see if you can improve it, using your partner's comments and the checklist on page 52.

What have you learnt?

During this chapter you have been learning the kinds of skills you need to demonstrate in order to meet the assessment criteria for GCSE. Working with a partner, go back through the things you have learnt and write three pieces of advice for someone just about to start their study of Reading Creative Texts.

- What are the three most important skills they need to demonstrate and how can they demonstrate these skills?
- Share your ideas with the class. Which skills were mentioned most often?

Check your progress

In this chapter you have learnt about how writers create character through their use of language, structure, form and narrative perspective. You have also looked at how to write effectively about characterisation, using analysis vocabulary and embedded evidence.

Taking it further

Read the lists in the boxes below. Which Level do you think you have reached in this chapter, and what do you need to do to improve?

LEVEL 5 (Aiming for GCSE C/B)

AF3 I can begin to make inferences and deductions based on textual evidence.

AF5 I can identify and explain various features of writers' use of language with some awareness of effects.

AF6 I can clearly identify a writer's purpose and viewpoint through general overview with some limited explanation of the effect on reader.

LEVEL 6 (Aiming for GCSE B/A)

AF3 I can make comments that are securely based in textual evidence and identify different layers of meaning with some attempt at detailed exploration.

AF5 I can offer some detailed explanation, with appropriate terminology, of how language is used, and comment on the overall effect on reader.

AF6 I can precisely identify a writer's purpose and viewpoint and clearly identify the effect on the reader with close reference to the text.

LEVEL 7 (Aiming for GCSE A/A*)

AF3 I can develop an interpretation of the text, making connections between different insights.

AF5 I can analyse how language is used precisely and perceptively with appreciation of the overall effect on the reader.

AF6 I can analyse a writer's purpose and viewpoint, developing an appreciation of how particular techniques and devices achieve the effects they do.

Next steps to GCSE

For GCSE, you will study a range of creative texts. You will analyse writers' craft in detail, considering how language, structure and form are used to present characters and ideas to the reader. You will also start to consider the social, cultural and historical context of the texts you read.

Chapter 3

Reading poetry

In this chapter you will read a range of challenging poems about people and their relationships to nature. You will explore the meanings of poems and the techniques used by poets to express their ideas.

Bridge to GCSE

To get you ready for your GCSE course, this chapter will take you through the following steps:

Explore ideas
- Learn how to write about and analyse poets' craft.
- Learn to use evidence like a GCSE student.

Check your skills
- Learn how to compare poems.

Extend your skills
- Learn how to structure a piece of analytical writing.

Plan and write
- Plan a written response and write effectively under timed conditions.

Improve your work
- Review your response and set yourself a target for improvement.

Your GCSE-style assessment task will be a one-hour timed analysis of a poem.

Key Stage 3 Reading Assessment Focuses		GCSE English Literature Assessment Objectives	
AF2	Understand, describe, select or retrieve information, events or ideas from texts and use quotation and reference to texts	AO1	Respond to texts critically and imaginatively; select and evaluate relevant textual detail to illustrate and support interpretations
AF4	Identify and comment on the structure and organisation of texts, including grammatical and presentational features at text level	AO2	Explain how language, structure and form contribute to writers' presentation of ideas, themes and settings
AF5	Explain and comment on writers' use of language, including grammatical and literary features at word and sentence level	AO3	Make comparisons and explain links between texts, evaluating writers' different ways of expressing meaning and achieving effects
AF6	Identify and comment on writers' purposes and viewpoints, and the overall effect of the text on the reader		

What is a poem?

Learning objective

- To learn how to approach a new poem for the first time.

Bridge to GCSE

- At GCSE it is important to be a confident, independent reader of a range of poetry.

Poetry has been around for thousands of years, since human beings were first able to use language. And, for much of that time, people have tried to answer the question: What is a poem?

Getting you thinking

1 With a partner, read and discuss the following definitions of poetry. Which ones are your favourites?

- Poetry is when an emotion has found its thought and the thought has found words. *Robert Frost*
- Poetry is ordinary language raised to the nth power. *Paul Engle*
- Poetry is thoughts that breathe, and words that burn. *Thomas Gray*
- The language beneath the language; that is poetry. *Andrea Pacione*
- Poetry is the best words in the best order. *Samuel Taylor Coleridge*
- Poetry gives you permission to feel. *James Autry*
- Poetry is the rhythmical creation of beauty in words. *Edgar Allan Poe*
- Poetry is the art of uniting pleasure with truth. *Samuel Johnson*

2 Either working with a partner or by yourself, write your own definition of poetry. You can use any ideas from the list of quotations to help you create your own definition.

Write your definition on a sticky note or in your exercise book. Share your definition with the class – can you reach a group definition?

3 Now, read the following statements. Which ones do you agree with?

- Poetry is hard to define.
- Poetry doesn't have to rhyme.
- Poetry is a way of communicating feelings and ideas through language and structure.
- The shape, form and language of a poem are vital to its meaning.

GCSE skills focus

Much poetry can be categorised as either 'lyric' (shorter poems which express personal feelings, ideas and themes) or 'narrative' – longer poems which tell a story.

Lyric poetry often explores a feeling, idea or theme by looking at something specific – an incident, a place, a person, an object, a memory. Most of the poetry you will study at GCSE will be lyric poetry, although you may read some examples of narrative or epic poetry.

Poets use some of the same techniques as writers of novels, short stories or even advertisements. However, poetry also has some particular, unique features. It is useful to develop a vocabulary to be able to talk about these features. Understanding them will make you a more confident, skilful poetry reader.

Poets want you to bring your own ideas and interpretations to their work. As you become more familiar and confident with poetry, you'll find it easier to ask yourself questions like these when you read a new poem:

- What is the poem about?

- How does it make me feel?

- What do I notice about the feelings, ideas or themes?

- How has the poet used language?

- What techniques has the poet used to present his or her ideas?

Bridge to GCSE

GCSE questions want you to explore **what** ideas and feelings are conveyed by a poem and **how** they are conveyed.

'Technique spotting' gets you no higher than a grade E at GCSE. You will need to explain (or even better, analyse) why the poet has used that technique – how it links to the feelings, ideas and themes conveyed in the poem.

Now you try it

Read the following poem a few times. Your first reading will probably be silently, to yourself. Try to hear the poem – the sounds, the patterns, the rhythms – in your head. It may also help to also read it aloud, either to yourself or with a partner.

The Storm

Without warning a snake of black
cloud rises in the sky.
It hisses as it runs and spreads its hood.
The moon goes out, the mountain is dark.
Far away is heard the shout of the demon.

Up rushes the storm a moment after
Rattling an iron chain in its teeth.
The mountain suddenly lifts its
Trunk to the heavens
And the lake roars like a wild beast.

Ashok B Raha

1 Either on your own or with a partner, answer these questions:
   - How does the poem make you feel about the storm?
   - Which words, phrases or images help you to hear and picture the storm?
   - What is the overall mood or tone of this poem?
   - How do you know that this is a poem?

2 The next area to explore is how the poet has communicated his or her ideas.

   The following table contains some of the techniques used in 'The Storm', along with their definitions. However, the definitions have been jumbled up. Copy and complete the table, putting the correct definition next to its term.

Top tip

If you get stuck, get a dictionary or go online to find out the correct definition. This is a useful site:

www.poetryarchive.org/ poetryarchive/glossaryIndex.do

You might want to start your own glossary of poetic terms.

Technique	Definition	Example from the poem	How it made me feel
Alliteration	Where an idea or thought (sentence or clause) carries on into the next line; sometimes called a run-on line		
Sibilance	An image in which one thing is compared to another using 'like' or 'as'		

Onomatopoeia	The treatment of an object or animal as though it had human feelings and qualities		
Personification	The use of words with the same starting sound placed near each other		
Simile	Where a word sounds like its meaning (e.g. 'rustle')		
Metaphor	The repetition of an 's' sound		
Enjambment	An image in which one thing stands for another in order to create a striking picture in the mind		

Taking it further

Now that you have identified the key techniques used in this poem, you need to analyse why these techniques have been used.

- Write a sentence explaining how the poet feels about the storm.
- Choose three of the techniques used in this poem.
- For each technique, write a sentence explaining how the poet uses this technique to present his feelings, ideas or themes.

You might start like this, for example:

> The poet feels that the storm is dangerous and threatening. He uses a metaphor, describing the storm as a 'snake of black cloud' to suggest ...

Top tip

Try to write three sentences about each technique rather than one. This way you will be developing your ability to analyse a technique.

Bridge to GCSE

Candidates who achieve the highest grades at GCSE analyse a small range of techniques in close detail, linking them to the overall effect and intention of the poem. Being able to write a 'lot about a little' is crucial for top grades.

What have you learnt?

Swap your work with a partner. Read their paragraph and give them:

- **one** mark for each technique mentioned
- **two** marks for a clear explanation of the poet's feelings about the storm
- **three** marks for each explanation of how the technique demonstrates the poet's feelings about the storm.

Check your level

LEVEL 5 I am aware of poets' choices of language and can identify them confidently.

LEVEL 6 I can make some detailed comments about the effects of particular word choices in poems.

LEVEL 7 I can make some insightful, detailed comments about the effects of particular word choices.

Learning objective

- To reinforce your understanding of how a poet uses structure and imagery to present their ideas.

Bridge to GCSE

- At GCSE being able to coment on a poem's structure and imagery is essential.

One of the great things about reading poetry is that there is always such a lot to discover. Once you know what clues to look for you can start to uncover different layers of meaning in the poem.

The imagery used by poets can create some wonderful pictures in the mind of the reader. Poets also use structure very deliberately to communicate their thoughts, feelings and ideas.

Getting you thinking

'Below the Green Corrie' explores the experience of walking in a favourite place in Scotland. Norman MacCaig has structured his poem in three stanzas.

Read the poem a few times and then answer the questions that follow.

Below the Green Corrie

The mountains gathered round me
like bandits. Their leader
swaggered up close in the dark light,
full of threats, full of thunders.

But it was they who stood and delivered.
They gave me their money and their lives.
They filled me with mountains and thunders.

My life was enriched
with an **infusion** of theirs.
I clambered downhill through the ugly weather.
And when I turned to look goodbye
to those marvellous prowlers
a sunshaft had pierced the clouds
and their leader,
that swashbuckling mountain,
was wearing
a **bandolier** of light.

Norman MacCaig

1 How does the poet feel at first when he climbs the mountains? Which words and phrases in the first stanza tell you this?

2 How do the poet's feelings change in the second stanza?

3 In the third stanza, what does the poet realise and take away from his experience?

Glossary

Infusion Extract of a substance's flavours (tea is an infusion, made from tea leaves).

Bandolier Belt with pockets for holding bullets.

GCSE skills focus

Thinking about the way a poet uses structure and organisation can help you to understand their ideas. If a poet has used stanzas to structure a poem, it is important to think about what is shown in each **stanza**.

Often metaphors are short. However, in 'Below the Green Corrie' the poet uses an extended metaphor throughout the poem. He compares the mountains to bandits to help explore his changing feelings towards the mountains and the natural world.

Key terms

Stanza A unit of a poem (a bit like a paragraph in prose) sometimes referred to as a verse (though this can be confusing as 'verse' is also another word for poetry).

Imagery is another very important poetic technique. Remember that a **metaphor** is where a poet compares something to something else in order to create a striking image in the mind of the reader.

Now you try it

Track the way the poet uses structure and imagery to show his changing feelings.

1 Complete the following table, commenting on what each piece of evidence suggests about the poet's feelings towards the mountains. You will notice that the evidence has been organised by stanza to help you think about how the poem's structure affects its meaning.

Stanza	Quotation from the poem	What this suggests about the poet's feelings
1	'The mountains gathered round me'	Suggests threat of being surrounded and trapped
1	'like bandits'	
1	'their leader swaggered'	
1	'up close'	
1	'full of threats, full of thunders'	
2	'But'	Uses a connective to signal a change in mood
2	'They gave me their money and their lives.'	
2	'They filled me with mountains and thunders.'	
3	'My life was enriched'	Sums up his change in attitude and positive feelings about the mountains
3	'marvellous prowlers'	
3	'that swashbuckling mountain'	
3	'bandolier of light'	

2 Use these ideas to write three paragraphs. You can use the following paragraph starters if you wish:

> In the first stanza, MacCaig feels threatened by the mountains. He compares them to...

> However, in the second stanza his opinion changes...

> In the final stanza MacCaig reflects on his experience and realises that ...

Checklist for success

✓ Use embedded evidence (short phrases or words from the poem that are inserted into your own sentences).

✓ Comment on the extended metaphor of bandits, explaining how and why MacCaig uses it.

✓ Finish by explaining what you think the experience meant to MacCaig.

Bridge to GCSE

Analysing means to go into lots of detail about the effects of particular words, phrases or techniques. If you can effectively write a 'lot about a little' then you are analysing.

Evaluating means considering the effectiveness of particular words, phrases or techniques. This is hard to do and you should avoid simply offering personal judgement on whether or not you like something.

Taking it further

'Lot about a little' analysis is one of the most important skills you can start to develop.

Take the phrase: *'Their leader swaggered up close'*.

Here's an example of some of the different points you could make about this phrase.

> Creates a sense of power and authority

> Feeling of claustrophobia – suggests that the mountains are moving towards him

> *'Their leader swaggered up close'*

> Confident, cocky, arrogant image

● Now, choose another phrase, line, or even just one word from the poem. Allow yourself five minutes to see how many ideas you can find to say about the section you have chosen.'

What have you learnt?

This is how one student commented on the phrase above:

> MacCraig creates an image of the mountains as not only being alive, but being 'bandits' that threaten him at first. In his description the 'leader' of the mountains appears to move: he 'swaggered up close'. This gives the impression that the speaker feels enclosed, claustrophobic and threatened. The 'swagger' of the 'leader' suggests his confidence and arrogance, as if the mountain is much more dangerous than the speaker and in control of the situation. He 'swagger[s] up close' as if he is in charge, invading the poet's personal space. This is very effective as an extended metaphor as it strongly suggests the way the speaker feels powerless in comparison to the natural world.

1 Read this sample and see if you can identify where the student
- uses embedded evidence
- comments on the effects of word choices
- comments on the feelings being presented
- goes into further detail about the effects of particular word choices
- mentions a specific technique
- comments on the purpose and effect of that technique
- evaluates the effectiveness of the metaphor without 'marking or grading' the poet.

2 Choose another phrase or line from the poem and write a paragraph of your own. Use the checklist to see if you can analyse ideas and language in the same way the student did.

3 Swap your paragraph with a partner. Award a Level based on the Levels in the box below.

Bridge to GCSE

Keep your focus clearly on how the poetic techniques are used to demonstrate the poet's feelings, ideas and themes.

Check your level

LEVEL 5   I can comment on some of the effects of structure and imagery.

LEVEL 6   I can explain in detail specific examples of structure and imagery.

LEVEL 7   I can analyse and evaluate in detail the overall effects of structure and imagery.

Learning objective

- To explore how to analyse the use of structure and form in poetry.

Bridge to GCSE

- At GCSE, learning to make comparisons and connections between poems is a really important skill.

To become expert readers of poetry for GCSE, you need to understand these terms:

- *theme* means the overall idea or point of the poem
- *viewpoint* means the poet's feelings, ideas, thoughts or perspective
- *interpretation* means your own understanding of the themes and ideas – in other words, your own 'reading' of the poem.

Poems can be understood in different ways. Once you get your head around this key concept you will be in a better position to explore and enjoy the layers of meaning within a poem.

Getting you thinking

Read the following poem out loud (remember the importance of *hearing* the poem).

Proud Songsters

The thrushes sing as the sun is going,
And the finches whistle in ones and pairs,
And as it gets dark loud nightingales
    In bushes
Pipe, as they can when April **wears**,
    As if all Time were theirs.

These are brand new birds of twelvemonths' growing,
Which a year ago, or less than **twain**,
No finches were, nor nightingales,
    Nor thrushes,
But only particles of grain,
    And earth, and air, and rain.

Thomas Hardy

Glossary

Wears Ends.
Twain Two.

1 Discuss with a partner your interpretation of this poem after reading it a couple of times.

- What is the poet's viewpoint?
- What is the theme of the poem?
- How does the poem make you feel?

2 Now look a little more closely at the structure of the poem.

- Could the first line be interpreted in more than one way?
- What about the last line – what is Hardy referring to in this list?
- Is there a change of **tense**? What is the effect of this?
- What is the theme or idea of the first stanza?
- What is the theme or idea of the second stanza?

Key terms

Tense Verbs can be present, past or future tense.

GCSE skills focus

In **lyric poems** (see page 55) poets often explore 'big' ideas or themes through a close focus on something specific. Often a lyric poem will start with the particular and then relate it to the 'big' general idea later in the poem. It is really important to look at the structure of a lyric poem as it often helps to develop the theme or idea.

The following structural features are also important to notice:

- use, length and position of the lines
- the start, end and organisation of each stanza (if the poem is organised into stanzas)
- enjambment (run-on lines)
- tense (past/present/future).

Now you try it

Student responses

1 Have a look at these initial student responses to the feelings, ideas and themes in Hardy's poem. When you have read them all, work in groups to decide which responses are most successful in how they have

- used detail to support their arguments
- described form, structure or language
- begun to explore the wider themes of the poem.

Share your findings with the rest of the class.

a This is a poem about listening to birds singing as it gets dark.

b The poet admires the birds — you can tell that from the title of the poem.

c The first stanza of the poem seems to focus on the bird song and the second stanza is more wide and general — as if the poet is using the description of the birdsong to make a bigger point about life and nature.

d This poem is about how all of nature is connected and this makes it powerful and beautiful. He uses the present tense in the first stanza to describe the birds — perhaps to suggest that it feels like they have been there forever. This would link to the ideas he is exploring.

e I like the way the list of birds in the second stanza links to the list of earth 'elements' — this really brings home the connection between the birds and the earth itself.

2 In 'Proud Songsters' the 'big' idea *might* be that everything in the world is connected to a larger life force. Hardy focuses on birdsong in particular to explore this idea.

However there are several other possible interpretations of the poem. Discuss whether you think it could also be suggesting ideas about

- the shortness or transience of life
- how magical and mysterious nature is that it can create these birds as if out of nothing.

Are there any other interpretations you can think of?

Look at how a student has communicated her ideas about this lyric poem:

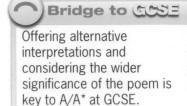

Bridge to GCSE

Offering alternative interpretations and considering the wider significance of the poem is key to A/A* at GCSE.

Hardy suggests that there is a connection between all living things. He presents this idea by describing birdsong and noticing how it sounds like it has always been there. He starts with a simple description of the birdsong, listing the birds he can hear and commenting that it sounds like they have always been there: 'as if all Time were theirs'. In the next stanza he brings in the idea of 'grain, and earth, and air, and rain' as if to suggest that the birds have come from the earth itself and will return to it. Using the present tense to describe the birdsong reinforces the idea that they are as much a part of the natural cycle of life as the 'air and rain', as if everything is ongoing. Furthermore, using the same listing technique to describe the range of birds and the elements highlights the connection between them. The wider significance of this is possibly a suggestion that we should be comforted by this because we are all part of something bigger.

— Sums up the overall point, demonstrating an overview of the main ideas

— Close attention to the structure of the poem

— Effective use of embedded evidence

— Analysis of the order of ideas and use of tense and listing, relating techniques to the poet's ideas and purpose

— Exploring ideas

The teacher annotations demonstrate how the student has achieved Level 7 in their response.

Taking it further

Here is another lyric poem which explores a similar theme to 'Proud Songsters'.

A Day in Autumn

It will not always be like this,
The air windless, a few last
Leaves adding their decoration
To the trees' shoulders, braiding the cuffs
Of the boughs with gold; a bird preening

In the lawn's mirror. Having looked up
From the day's chores, pause a minute,
Let the mind take its photograph
Of the bright scene, something to wear
Against the heart in the long cold.

RS Thomas

1 Read the poem a few times and discuss these key questions:

● What is the overall mood or tone of the poem?
● What might the poet be suggesting in the first line?
● What do you notice about the use of metaphors? Are they positive or negative?
● What kind of feeling do you get from the last two lines?
● Does the poem follow the structure of a lyric poem in the way it moves from the particular to a bigger idea?

2 Use the ideas generated from your discussion to make some brief notes in response to the questions.

> **Bridge to GCSE**
>
> The poet's 'viewpoint' is the term for the attitude or point of view being presented. Sometimes the poet's viewpoint can be different to the speaker's viewpoint, so be careful when you consider this.

What have you learnt?

Using your notes, complete your own response to 'A Day in Autumn'. It is important to comment on the poet's viewpoint.

Checklist for success

✓ Write 300–400 words.
✓ Use supporting evidence embedded in your sentences.
✓ Comment on the use of language, structure and form.
✓ Focus clearly on *how* the poet presents his feelings/ideas/themes.

Check your level

LEVEL 5 I can identify and explain what the poem is about and the main viewpoint of the poet.

LEVEL 6 I can explore how the use of form and structure links to the poem's meanings and ideas.

LEVEL 7 I can analyse and evaluate how the poet has used form and structure to communicate their ideas.

Learning objective

- To develop ways of exploring the overall feelings, ideas or themes in a poem.
- To learn how to make links and comparisons between poems.

Bridge to GCSE

- At GCSE you will consider the difference between theme and content, forming a deeper understanding of how poets present their ideas.

Poets can use a topic, or story, or character to present their main theme or idea. So, when you read a poem, there may be two answers to the question: *What is this poem about?*

- It might, for example, be about a young married couple who are living in an unfamiliar part of the world.
- It might also be about the way that society treats outsiders.

In other words, the content of the poem often demonstrates the theme.

Getting you thinking

Remember the 'first response' questions that help you explore a poem when you read it for the first time (see page 55).

1 Read the poem below, by Vernon Scannell.

Bridge to GCSE

You can access a poem on many levels – you don't have to understand every word in order to respond successfully. GCSE students often respond to the same poem in a variety of different ways.

Nettles

My son aged three fell in the nettle bed.
'Bed' seemed a curious name for those green spears,
That regiment of spite behind the shed:
It was no place for rest. With sobs and tears
The boy came seeking comfort and I saw
White blisters beaded on his tender skin.
We soothed him till his pain was not so raw.
At last he offered us a watery grin,
And then I took my billhook, honed the blade
And went outside and slashed in fury with it
Till not a nettle in that fierce parade
Stood upright any more. Next task: I lit
A funeral pyre to burn the fallen dead.
But in two weeks the busy sun and rain
Had called up tall recruits behind the shed:
My son would often feel sharp wounds again.

Vernon Scannell

2 In pairs, discuss your ideas about the following questions:

- How does the father feel about his son?
- How does he feel about the nettles?
- Why does he react the way he does to the nettles?

3 Did you notice that there seems to be an **extended metaphor** running through the whole poem?

- What is this extended metaphor?
- Why do you think the poet might have chosen to use it in this poem?
- Write down all the words or phrases related to this extended metaphor.

Key terms

Extended metaphor Term for a key image which is repeated throughout a poem for deliberate effect. Sometimes called a 'conceit'.

GCSE skills focus

Comparing texts is an important part of GCSE English and English Literature. There are many ways of making links and finding comparisons between poems, including looking at

- feelings, ideas and themes
- topic or subject-matter
- structure, form and organisation
- language and imagery

Now you try it

Read the poem 'Thistles' by Ted Hughes.

Thistles

Against the rubber tongues of cows and the **hoeing** hands of men
Thistles spike the summer air
Or crackle open under a blue-black pressure

Every one a revengeful burst
Of **resurrection**, a grasped fistful
Of splintered weapons and Icelandic frost thrust up

From the underground stain of a decayed Viking.
They are like pale hair and the **gutturals** of **dialects**.
Every one manages a plume of blood.

Then they grow grey, like men.
Mown down, it is a feud. Their sons appear,
Stiff with weapons, fighting back over the same ground.

Ted Hughes

Glossary

Hoeing Breaking up the surface of the soil to destroy little weeds.

Resurrection Coming back to life.

Gutturals sounds from the back of the throat, such as the hard 'g' sound.

Dialects Regional languages, based on a formal language such as English but with some of their own words and pronunciations.

- What do you think 'Thistles' is about? Is there a broad idea or theme running through it?
- Just as you did with 'Nettles', find all the words or phrases related to 'war' in 'Thistles'.
- Who is doing the 'feuding' in the poem?
- What mood does this poem convey?
- Which particular words and phrases suggest this mood?

Bridge to GCSE

Get into the habit of making links and cross-references between the poems you read. You will often have to compare at least two poems – either in an exam or a controlled assessment.

Taking it further

1 Working with a partner, choose one or two lines from 'Nettles' and write them on a sheet of A4 paper. Choose one or two lines from 'Thistles' and also write them on your sheet of paper.

2 You now have five minutes to fill your sheet of paper. Write down anything at all that the lines you have chosen suggest to you.

You might include:
- the effects of particular words/phrases
- what particular words make you think of or remind you of
- any techniques you notice
- any links between the ideas or themes in the two poems.

3 When your five minutes is up, swap your sheet of A4 paper with another pair.

You now have another five minutes to read their notes and add as much as you can to their sheet of paper. Remember, they will possibly have chosen different lines from the two poems, so be prepared to work quickly.

Return your sheets to each other. Your original sheet should now contain both your original thoughts and some ideas from the others.

4 Copy and complete the table on the next page to help you to understand some of the similarities and differences between the poems. Tick to indicate which poem is being referred to.

Point	'Nettles'	'Thistles'
This poem is about a father who wants to protect his son from the pain of life.		
This poem is about the power of nature and how it is never going to be controlled by humans.		
The poet uses an extended metaphor of war to suggest the way humans fight to control the earth.		
The poet uses an extended metaphor of war to highlight his desperation to protect his son from harm.		

You will have noticed that one of the main links between these two poems is the ways the poets both use metaphor.

5 Complete the following sentences by turning them into a complete paragraph which compares the two poems:

- In 'Nettles', Scannell uses an extended metaphor of war with words like ...
- In 'Thistles', Hughes also uses an extended metaphor with words like ...
- Both poets suggest that the plants are ...
- Both poets also seem to feel that nature is ...
- However, a key difference between the poems is that 'Nettles' is about ...
- Whereas, on the other hand, 'Thistles' is about ...

What have you learnt?

You should now have a paragraph which describes some of the techniques, themes and ideas in the poems, and uses evidence to back up your points. Use the list below to check your work, and write a second, improved version if necessary.

Checklist for success

✓ Comment on the techniques used in the two poems.
✓ Give specific examples of the techniques.
✓ Use embedded evidence.
✓ Compare the similarities between the poems.
✓ Contrast the differences between the poems.
✓ Focus on feelings, attitudes and ideas rather than just techniques.

Check your level

LEVEL 4	I can understand the difference between theme and content in at least one poem.
LEVEL 5	I can explain the theme of the poem and how the content links to the theme.
LEVEL 6	I can start to explore the themes of both poems and construct a confident comparison between them.

Learning objective

- To learn how to link smaller points to a central thesis or overview when you produce a written response to poetry.

Bridge to GCSE

- At GCSE being able to present a confident overview of a text is key to securing high marks.

Poets don't usually sit down to write a poem with a checklist of techniques they want to include in their work. Their reason for writing a poem is a point they want to make, or a feeling, theme or idea they want to explore.

Getting to grips with an overview of the poet's intention and purpose is the best starting point for writing about a poem. Being able to consider this overview in your work will enable you to present a structured, coherent response to the poem.

Getting you thinking

Storm on the Island

We are prepared: we build our houses squat,
Sink walls in rock and roof them with good slate.
The wizened earth has never troubled us
With hay, so, as you can see, there are no **stacks**
Or **stooks** that can be lost. Nor are there trees
Which might prove company when it blows full
Blast: you know what I mean – leaves and branches
Can raise a tragic chorus in a gale
So that you can listen to the thing you fear
Forgetting it pummels your house too.
But there are no trees, no natural shelter.
You might think that the sea is company,
Exploding comfortably down on the cliffs
But no: when it begins, the flung spray hits
The very windows, spits like a tame cat
Turned savage. We just sit tight while wind dives
And **strafes** invisibly. Space is a **salvo**.
We are bombarded by the empty air.
Strange, it is a huge nothing that we fear.

Seamus Heaney

Annotations:
- Does this sound confident? Effect of first-person plural?
- Double meaning?
- What does this suggest about trying to farm the island?
- Why is the word 'company' repeated?
- What does this image evoke?
- Effect?
- Effect of sibilance and rhyme with hits?
- What is the effect of this reflection?

Glossary

Stacks Haystacks.
Stooks Piles of sheaves of corn.
Strafes Attacks repeatedly with bombs or machine-gun fire from aircraft.
Salvo Simultaneous firing of weapons.

- Jot down some brief answers, in note form, to the questions and points raised in the annotations.

GCSE skills focus

Earlier in this chapter you learned how to identify and analyse writers' techniques in detail. The next stage is to link these techniques to a central **thesis** or overview which summarises the writer's overall themes, ideas and viewpoints.

Use your annotations and ideas to develop and explore the thesis: *Heaney is presenting existence on the island as a grim battle between humanity and nature.*

Key terms

Thesis Central idea in an essay or argument which may be proved, disproved or partially proved through discussion.

Now you try it

Make some notes in response to the following questions:

- What is the effect of Heaney's use of pronouns (we, you, I, it)?

- How does Heaney explore the idea of loneliness and isolation?

- Heaney uses an extended metaphor. What is the metaphor and how does it portray the different sides in the battle? Which side seems to be the stronger and why? What does this tell us about Heaney's viewpoint about nature?

Bridge to GCSE

Developing an overview and then exploring and analysing how a writer uses language and structure or form to present their feeling, ideas and themes is key to Grade A/A* at GCSE.

2 Have a look at these two essay openings:

Student A

In 'Storm on the Island', Heaney describes a powerful storm hitting an isolated island. Heaney is on the island when the storm starts.

Heaney shows that the humans know the storm will be bad because they get ready for it. He says 'we are prepared' and that the houses are built in 'rock' and the roofs are made of 'good slate'.

Student B

Heaney creates a powerful sense of living very close to dangerous nature in 'Storm on the Island'. He contrasts nervous, isolated people with a powerful and destructive storm to suggest that life on the island is a grim battle for survival. The speaker of the poem is present on the island as the storm breaks.

The opening of the poem possibly suggests the speaker's lack of confidence. At first sight, the word 'squat' seems to suggest that the houses are built low and sturdy to help withstand the wind and fits in with the idea that they 'are prepared'. However, it could also imply that the speaker is aware that humans do not belong on the island and that they are squatters waiting to be evicted by the island's rightful owner – nature. This links in with the fact that nature provides no 'company' in the form of trees or support – 'the wizened earth has never troubled us with hay'.

Which opening is more effective and why? Use what you have learned so far in this chapter to write a commentary on each student's response.

Think about

- how effective each opening sentence is at introducing the key ideas of the poem
- how well each student has demonstrated their understanding of the key ideas
- how each student has commented on the use of language in the poem
- how each student has used evidence to support their ideas.

Taking it further

An effective plan for a written response to poetry needs to

- refer to the thesis or central idea in each part of the plan so that it can be developed effectively through the essay
- link each paragraph together.

Look at the following plan for the writing task:

How does Heaney present humans and nature in 'Storm on the Island?

Paragraph 1	Heaney uses pronouns to create a variety of effects.
Paragraph 2	Heaney emphasises the isolation of the speaker. Develop ideas from paragraph 1 but write about different techniques.
Paragraph 3	Heaney uses a violent extended metaphor of an air raid. Develop idea that nature is more powerful and 'winning' the battle.
Conclusion	Return to the question and try to link separate ideas into a new point.

1 Working in a group of four, each take one of the four paragraphs. Allow yourselves 10 minutes to write your section of this 'essay'.

2 When all four of you have finished, swap your work until each member of your group has read each of the sections. Allow five minutes for feedback and discussion on how to improve each other's sections.

Checklist for success

✓ Explain and develop the thesis clearly and concisely in the introduction. Time spent getting this right at the start will make the rest of the essay easier.

✓ Embed quotations in your sentences. This will help you to write more concisely and also shows that you understand the quotation implicitly (without having to spell it out).

✓ Refer to the writer by using their last name: in this case, 'Heaney'. This will help you to focus on the writer's techniques and viewpoint.

What have you learnt?

Swap essays with another group and highlight examples of the following:

● use of the writer's last name
● embedded quotations
● connectives used to link, explore and develop ideas
● three examples of sentences which develop the central thesis.

What could your partner group do to improve their essay?

Check your level

LEVEL 6	I can explain the effects of particular words and techniques in some detail.
LEVEL 7	I can analyse the effects of particular words and techniques, making links between ideas.
LEVEL 8	I can show clearly how language has been used to support the writer's purpose.

Learning objective

● To focus in detail on identifying which ideas to write about.

● To plan how to use these ideas in a structured, organised written response to poetry.

Bridge to GCSE

● At GCSE you will need to be able to plan and write an effective response to a new poem.

Depending on which GCSE English or English Literature course you follow, there are a number of ways you could be assessed for poetry.

You might

● **produce a detailed controlled assessment response, focusing on several poems**

● **compare some poems with other forms of text such as prose fiction or Shakespeare in a controlled assessment**

● **compare some previously studied poems (usually two) in an examination**

● **respond to a previously unseen poem in an examination.**

Your task

Your assessment task for this chapter will be to respond to the following question:

> *How do the speaker's feelings about relationships change in response to nature in the poem 'Winter Swans'?*

You should aim to write at least two sides of A4. You will be given up to one hour to complete this task.

Read the poem on page 75. Remember to read actively, preferably more than once, and aloud if possible.

Make some notes or annotate a copy of the poem. Remember to ask yourself:

● What is this poem about? What is the content or subject matter?

● What are the feelings, ideas and themes?

● What techniques has Sheers used to express his feelings, ideas or themes?

Winter Swans

The clouds had given their all –
two days of rain and then a break
in which we walked,

the waterlogged earth
gulping for breath at our feet
as we skirted the lake, silent and apart,

until the swans came and stopped us
with a show of tipping in unison.
As if rolling weights down their bodies to their heads

they halved themselves in the dark water,
icebergs of white feather, paused before returning again
like boats righting in rough weather.

'They mate for life' you said as they left,
porcelain over the stilling water. I didn't reply
but as we moved on through the afternoon light,

slow-stepping in the lake's shingle and sand,
I noticed our hands, that had, somehow,
swum the distance between us
and folded, one over the other,
like a pair of wings settling after flight.

Owen Sheers

GCSE skills focus

You are going to explore some ways of organising your thoughts about 'Winter Swans'.

- Use of imagery – 'dark water', 'icebergs'
- Negative ideas – 'gulped for breath, 'given their all'
- Use of structure – starts negatively 'silent and apart', ends positively with joined hands
- **Feelings about relationships/natural world**
- Positive ideas – change of weather, 'afternoon light',
- Links between humans and swans – 'swum the distance', 'settling after flight'

- Use this spider diagram as a starting point for your own.
See how many ideas you can add.

- Once you have gathered some ideas, you need to think about the structure and organisation of your written response.

Here is an example of how one student has planned an essay.

The plan

- uses the introduction to provide 'hooks' to hang ideas onto
- answers the question
- links each paragraph to the main idea
- returns to the question at the end, showing how the question has been answered
- focuses on feelings, ideas and themes
- focuses on how language and poetic techniques demonstrate the feelings, ideas and themes.

The notes provide a useful model of how to structure and organise your ideas.

Bridge to GCSE

Getting into good habits of structure and organisation now will help you enormously with your GCSE work.

Introduction
Use some key words from the question: 'nature', 'feelings about relationships'
Answer the question: explain what aspect of natural world Sheers uses (swans), explain his feelings about relationships (starts negatively, ends positively)
Introduce the idea that the swans bring the couple back together again, suggests that humans can learn lessons from the beauty and simplicity of the natural world
Paragraph 2
Topic sentence – negative feelings at start of poem
How this is presented – 'given their all', 'clouds', 'silent and apart', 'gulped for breath' etc
Developing paragraph
Topic sentence – the links between the swans and their relationship
How this is presented – 'came and stopped us', 'show of tipping in unison', 'boats righting in rough weather'
Further development
Topic sentence – how the experience changes them
How this is presented – comparison between the couple and the swans with language like 'swum', 'folded', 'wings'
Conclusion/wider idea
Lessons to be learned from the natural world, the beauty and simplicity of nature, the idea that humans over-complicate things perhaps?

Plan your response

Structure your essay carefully to develop all the points you want to make, in a clear and logical order. Key structural elements are:

- the introduction, which sets out the argument you will develop
- topic sentences, which begin each paragraph in the main part of the essay
- the conclusion, which completes the argument you have developed, drawing points together.

A coherently structured essay should make sense if a reader just reads the introduction, each topic sentence and the conclusion.

f your topic sentence of each paragraph is right, it will be easier to explore and develop ideas in the rest of the paragraph.

Think of a topic sentence as the 'subheading' of each paragraph. t also introduces the main point of the paragraph.

1 Look back at the student's plan. He or she has decided to write about 'negative feelings' in the second paragraph.

Which of the following two topic sentences is going to allow the student to develop his or her ideas most effectively?

> 1 There are negative feelings at the start of the poem.
> 2 Sheers uses the natural world to explore the negative feelings between the couple at the beginning of the poem.

Uses writer's second name

Links to question

Links to question

Begins to show awareness of structure

2 Using the second topic sentence, turn the list of ideas below into a really good paragraph of analysis:

- negative use of language at the start: 'clouds'
- 'given their all' suggests the couple are giving up   as if they have been trying too hard
- Sheers is describing the weather as a metaphor for their relationship.

Bridge to GCSE

Remember the importance of writing 'a lot about a little'. Explore one or two key ideas in detail.

Write your response

Now it's time to complete your own plan, and then write your essay:

How do the speaker's feelings about relationships change in response to nature in the poem 'Winter Swans'?

Use a spider diagram and a written structure like the student's plan above, to plan your work in detail before you start.

Focus on the points on the right to get higher marks.

Checklist for success

✓ Demonstrate your understanding of feelings, ideas and themes.

✓ Analyse how the poet has presented their feelings, ideas or themes through language and structure.

✓ Summarise your ideas in the introduction – answer the question and provide 'hooks' for your ideas.

✓ Make sure you link the techniques to the meaning (no 'technique-spotting').

✓ 'Lot about a little' analysis will get you higher marks.

✓ Try to organise your paragraphs clearly, using topic sentences to introduce each new idea or area of focus.

Reading and reflecting

Learning objective

● To consider how to use assessment to improve your own work.

Bridge to GCSE

● At GCSE, being able to evaluate your own work is important to achieving the best marks.

Sometimes it is easier to assess work by other students rather than your own. When you get to GCSE you will continually look back at your work and find ways of making it better, so getting into good habits now will really help you in the future. Look at how one student has approached this assessment task first of all, then apply the same criteria to your own work.

Getting you thinking

Aafi is a Year 9 student. Here is part of his essay – he is focusing on the way the poet has created a negative tone and mood in the poem.

The first line of the poem creates a sad mood straight away. The second word is 'cloud', which seems gloomy and dull, and this is followed with 'given their all'. This gives the reader the idea that something or someone has given up or been defeated in some way. However, when you have read the poem and come back to this line there is another way the line could be interpreted: as if clouds have given their all – rain – must mean the bad weather is over. However, you don't know this when you read the poem for the first time.

He then describes the earth as 'waterlogged' which sounds as if the earth is trapped somehow, and suggests claustrophobia. This is reinforced with 'gulping for breath', a metaphor to suggest the sound of the couple's feet but also struggle and exertion. He is referring to their relationship at the same time as he is referring to the earth, linking their feelings to nature. The word 'skirted' gives a sense that the couple are avoiding not only the lake but each other and possibly the problems they are facing. This is supported by the adjectives 'silent and apart'.

GCSE skills focus

In this chapter you have been learning to

- respond to writers' feelings, attitudes, ideas and meanings
- focus on how writers' techniques link to their overall meaning and purpose
- structure and organise a response, linking paragraphs logically and coherently
- create an overview in an essay
- analyse evidence effectively and embed it in your answers
- use analysis vocabulary to create a sophisticated style.

Using this list, comment on Aafi's work, suggesting ways in which he might improve it.

Now you try it

Now read your own response again. Highlight any points where you have successfully applied the skills developed in the chapter. When you have finished, write a comment on how your work could be improved, using the checklist on page 80 to help you.

Taking it further

When you get to GCSE it is important to have a clear understanding of the ways you are being assessed. You will need to demonstrate that you

- have a detailed understanding of the themes and ideas
- can explain and analyse how the writer has communicated their themes and ideas.

To demonstrate these skills you will need to

- write in a clear, organised and purposeful way
- using well-chosen, appropriate evidence
- compare texts in interesting ways.

1 Read your assessment task again. Choose one section where you feel you could add one more paragraph in order to demonstrate these skills. This might be another paragraph analysing some particular language features, or a more detailed introduction.

2 Write your paragraph. When you have finished, swap with a partner and see what they think. Does the new paragraph improve your assessment task? Does their new paragraph improve their work?

Check your progress

In this chapter you have planned and written a timed assessment task on poetry, focusing on how a writer uses language, structure and form. You have learned about the importance of structuring your own ideas and why writing a 'lot about a little' is such an important skill.

Taking it further

Read the points under each Level heading below. Which Level do you think you have reached in this chapter, and what do you need to do to improve?

LEVEL 5 (Aiming for GCSE C/B)

AF2 I can identify relevant points and support them with relevant textual reference or quotation.

AF4 I can comment on structure and organisation and show awareness of writers' craft.

AF5 I can identify and explain various features of writers' use of language with some awareness of the effects of these choices.

AF6 I can identify the writer's main purpose and viewpoint with some explanation of the effect on the reader.

LEVEL 6 (Aiming for GCSE B/A)

AF2 I can clearly identify relevant points and support them with apt textual reference to support my ideas and arguments.

AF4 I can demonstrate some detailed exploration of how structural choices support writers' themes and purposes.

AF5 I can give some detailed explanation, with appropriate terminology, of how language is used, with comments on the overall effects on reader.

AF6 I can confidently identify the writer's main purpose and effects on the reader.

LEVEL 7 (Aiming for GCSE A/A*)

AF2 I can select precise and relevant textual references to illustrate my points.

AF4 I can evaluate the effects of structural and organisational choices linked to themes and purposes.

AF5 I can analyse precisely how language is used with appreciation of effects on reader.

AF6 I can analyse and evaluate writers' purposes, developing an appreciation of how particular techniques and devices achieve the effects they do.

Next steps to GCSE

For GCSE, you will be applying these skills to a range of poetry. You will also further develop your comparison skills, making connections between contemporary poems and poems from the past. You will analyse how poets use language, structure and form to convey their ideas, and consider how the *context* of the poetry affects its meaning.

Chapter 4

Exploring Shakespeare

In this chapter you will read the openings of two of Shakespeare's most famous plays, *Macbeth* and *Hamlet*. You will consider how Shakespeare uses the supernatural and language to grab the audience's attention and create powerful characters.

Bridge to GCSE

To get you ready for your GCSE course, this chapter will take you through the following steps:

Explore ideas

- Recognise the importance of the social and historical context of the plays.
- Analyse how Shakespeare creates effects through structure and language.

Check your skills

- Practise writing precisely and thoroughly about language and character.

Extend your skills

- Analyse different characters' responses to the supernatural.

Plan and write

- Plan and organise your ideas carefully to present your understanding of the plays effectively.

Improve your work

- Review your response and set yourself a target for improvement.

Your GCSE-style assessment task will be to compare the plays' openings.

Key Stage 3 Reading Assessment Focuses		GCSE English Literature Assessment Objectives	
AF2	Understand, describe, select or retrieve information, events or ideas from texts and use quotation and reference to text	AO1	Respond to texts critically and imaginatively; select and evaluate relevant textual detail to illustrate and support interpretations
AF4	Identify and comment on the structure and organisation of texts, including grammatical and presentational features at text level	AO3	Make comparisons and explain links between texts, evaluating writers' different ways of expressing meaning and achieving effects
AF5	Explain and comment on writers' use of language, including grammatical and literary features at word and sentence level	AO4	Relate texts to their social, cultural and historical contexts; explain how texts have been influential and significant to self and other readers in different contexts and at different times
AF7	Relate texts to their social, cultural and historical contexts		

1 The context of the plays

Learning objective

- To consider the meaning and impact of ghosts and historical beliefs about the supernatural and witches.

Bridge to GCSE

- At GCSE, you will need to demonstrate your understanding of the ideas and attitudes of Shakespeare's time, and link them to your comments on his plays.

In the plays *Macbeth* and *Hamlet*, Shakespeare uses the **supernatural** to catch the audience's attention, establish certain ideas and create a particular atmosphere. However, he didn't invent witches and ghosts: the idea of these strange beings has been around for much longer.

Key terms

Supernatural Strange and mysterious things, beyond the laws of nature, such as ghosts and witches, which have long fascinated and frightened people.

Getting you thinking

1 Working with a partner, begin by brainstorming what the idea of 'ghosts' means to you. Create a spider diagram that records anything and everything you know about ghosts, and also any films, books and plays you know in which ghosts appear.

2 Work with your partner to explore all the ideas you associate with 'witches'. Think about their appearance, their powers, where they appear in today's culture and anything else they suggest to you. Together, write a definition of both ghosts and witches.

GCSE skills focus

So far you have been considering a modern view of ghosts, but it is important to consider the context of Shakespeare's plays, which were written over four centuries ago. (*Hamlet* was written between 1599 and 1601; and *Macbeth* between 1603 and 1607.) Life was very different then, and so were people's understanding and beliefs about the world.

Key terms

Shakespeare wrote while there were two monarchs on the throne: Elizabeth I (1558–1603) and James I (1603–1625). These two periods in history are referred to as the **Elizabethan** era and the **Jacobean** era.

Witches were often blamed for terrible events, such as the bubonic plague. In a society dominated by men, and in an atmosphere of fear and anger, it was easy to blame disasters that couldn't be easily explained on women, usually those who were old, poor and single.

King James I believed in witches and had taken part in trials of witches. He wrote a serious book called *Daemonologie* about the dangers of the supernatural, including witches. The book included this advice on what to do if you encountered a ghost:

> Enter into no communication with suche spirites, neither aske them what thou must giue, or what thou must doo, or what shal happen hereafter. Aske them not who they are, or why they haue presented them selues to bee seene or hearde. For if they be good, they will lyke it well that thou wilte heare nothing but the woorde of God: but yf they be wicked, they wyll endeuour to deceyue thee with lying.

Another very popular book was *Of Ghostes and Spirites Walking by Nyght* by Lewes Lavater. This was a scientific enquiry into what ghosts are, and it assumes ghosts are real – as most Elizabethans and Jacobeans would have done.

> And diuers times it commeth to passe, that when some of our acquaintaunce or friends lye a dying, albeit they are some many miles off, yet there are some great stirrings or noises heard. sometimes we thinke the house will fall on our heads, or that some massie and waightie thing falleth downe throughout all the house, rendering and making a disordered noise: and shortlie within fewe months after, we vnderstande that those things happened, the very same houre that our friends departed in.

Now you try it

1 With this knowledge, think about how Shakespeare's audience might react to seeing a ghost (in *Hamlet*) or some witches (in *Macbeth*) appearing on the stage. Discuss, with your partner, what you think a typical theatre-goer would be thinking and feeling.

What would be the effects of putting ghosts and witches on stage and why might Shakespeare have done this?

2 A performance on stage is very different to a story being read, as it turns words into reality. Shakespeare's plays need the director and actors to bring the ghost or witches to life and create the atmosphere that goes with them.

Working in groups of three or four, create a short performance, which centres on a ghost. You are seeking to create a powerful and unsettling atmosphere, and you will need to make decisions about how you can effectively create the impression of a ghost.

Consider the following questions, and in each case how you are going to convey this to your audience:

- Where and when does the scene take place?
- Who is involved?
- How do you show the ghost?
  - What does the audience see or hear?
  - Does the ghost appear?
  - Are there 'signs' of a ghost?
- How do the other characters react to the ghost?
- How do they show this reaction?

Consider sound effects or special effects that you could use on a stage (although these may not be practical in a classroom).

Your piece should be just two or three minutes long, and does not need to be a polished performance. Perform your piece for the rest of the class. While you watch other groups' scenes, look for what you think is powerful and effective.

Bridge to GCSE

At GCSE, thinking for yourself and believing in your own ideas is essential to reaching the highest grades. Many students are afraid of being wrong – but think carefully and sensibly and your ideas will be valid.

Top tip

Remember that to create a disturbing atmosphere your performance must be convincing, not silly.

Taking it further

1 Once you have seen everyone's performance, make a list of the similarities you noticed.

2 Reflect on your own work and think about improvements to make it more powerful and atmospheric. Write a paragraph explaining the changes you would make and why you think these changes would heighten the impact on the audience.

3 Look at the image on the right, a woodcut from the fifteenth century. What does it tell us about how witches were perceived at this time?

What have you learnt?

You have been thinking about the ideas and context of *Macbeth* and *Hamlet*. Working with a partner, make a list of three key things you have identified about

- the supernatural
- beliefs and attitudes when Shakespeare was writing the plays
- how a theatre audience might react to seeing the supernatural on stage.

Compare your list with another pair, justifying the choices you have each made.

Check your level

LEVEL 5	I can make connections between when a text was written and what the text means.
LEVEL 6	I can explain how the ideas and meaning of a text are linked to its historical context.
LEVEL 7	I can discuss how the writer uses the beliefs of the time to make an impact on an audience.

Learning objective

- To explore and analyse the techniques Shakespeare uses to establish the tone and atmosphere of the plays.

Bridge to GCSE

- At GCSE you will explore how language and structure work and the effect they have on the reader.

Elizabethan theatre was a rowdy, popular place. People went to be entertained, and would eat, drink and talk during the performance – it was more like a rock concert than the theatre today, where people sit quietly and respectfully.

Shakespeare wanted to grab the audience's attention at the start of his plays. *Romeo and Juliet* begins with a big fight and *The Tempest* starts with a huge storm and shipwreck.

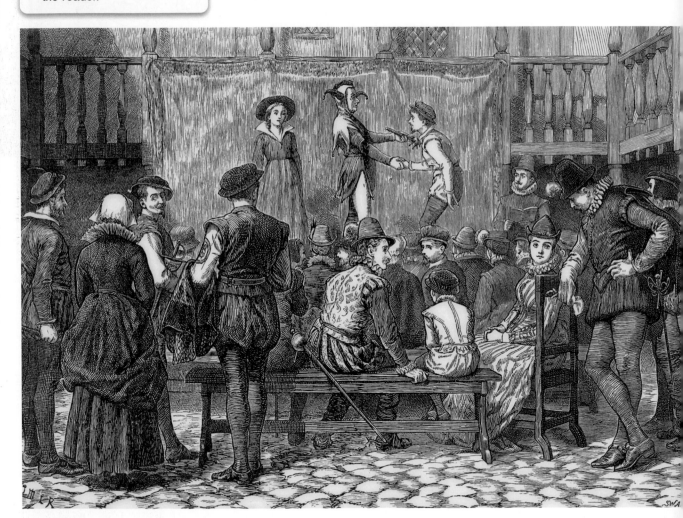

Getting you thinking

On the next page is the entire opening scene of *Macbeth*. Read it through and write down your first impressions – these are vitally important. Shakespeare has deliberately started the play in this way to establish a specific atmosphere.

Act 1 Scene 1. *A desert place*

Thunder and lightning. Enter three Witches

FIRST WITCH	When shall we three meet again In thunder, lightning, or in rain?
SECOND WITCH	When the hurlyburly's done, When the battle's lost and won.
THIRD WITCH	That will be ere the set of sun.
FIRST WITCH	Where the place?
SECOND WITCH	Upon the heath.
THIRD WITCH	There to meet with Macbeth.
FIRST WITCH	I come, **Graymalkin**!
SECOND WITCH	**Paddock** calls.
THIRD WITCH	Anon
ALL	Fair is foul, and foul is fair: Hover through the foul and filthy air.

Exeunt

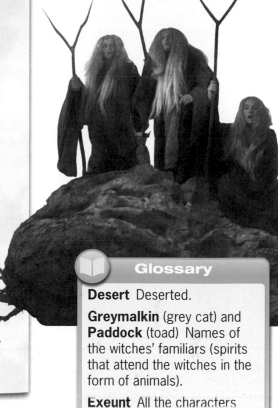

Glossary

Desert Deserted.

Greymalkin (grey cat) and **Paddock** (toad) Names of the witches' familiars (spirits that attend the witches in the form of animals).

Exeunt All the characters leave the stage.

GCSE skills focus

To write effectively about any piece of literature you need to explain **how** and **why** the writer has done something. This is analysis, and the more carefully and precisely you analyse the structure and language of the play, the more you will show your understanding of it.

It is easy to explain what happens in the first scene of *Macbeth*:

Three witches meet to decide when, where and why they will meet again: before sunset, on the heath, to meet Macbeth.

However, all this does is retell the story, which is a basic skill.

Instead, you need to analyse the choices Shakespeare has made in the opening scene to create a particular atmosphere – giving your explanation of how and why he has done something.

The first stage direction tells us that the scene is set in 'A desert place' (a deserted place). You need to be able to explain why Shakespeare chose this setting, rather than, say, a palace or a marketplace.

Top tip

The more thoughtfully and thoroughly you can analyse Shakespeare's choices and language, the more marks you will gain.

A good way to begin is by brainstorming the ideas you associate with the word 'deserted'. You could, for example, create a spider diagram of associations, as shown here.

These associations or **connotations** of the word are essential for effective analysis of a word and its effect.

You can use the ideas from your brainstorm to begin to analyse what Shakespeare has done. For example:

lonely

abandoned

barren

empty

hidden

deserted

isolated

forbidding

derelict

unpleasant

desolate

> Shakespeare sets the first scene of Macbeth in 'A desert place' because he wants to create a lonely and unpleasant atmosphere. This puts the audience on edge, making them nervous right from the start, wondering what might happen in an empty and abandoned place like this.

Top tip

The more you practise thinking about the meanings and connotations of words, the better you will get at it. Soon you should be able to brainstorm the associations in your head.

Now you try it

The next piece of information Shakespeare gives us is 'Thunder and lightning'.

1 Brainstorm the associations of this yourself. How many different ideas and connotations can you think of?

2 Select the words and ideas that you think are most helpful in explaining why Shakespeare chose this kind of weather to start the play. Use these to write your own analysis.

3 Swap your analysis with your partner, read what he or she has written, then try to add another sentence to the comment to make it even more detailed.

Next, Shakespeare introduces the first characters the audience see in *Macbeth*, 'Enter three Witches'. Think carefully about the impact of these three figures on the audience.

Top tip

Remember the introduction to this lesson, and that thunder and lightning would have been created by what were cutting-edge special effects – rolling a cannonball down a wooden trough for thunder and fireworks for lightning.

4 Look carefully at the picture of the witches, above, from a production of *Macbeth*. Jot down your thoughts on their appearance, what they are wearing, how you think they might move on stage, what you think their voices might sound like. Remind yourself of the work you did in the previous lesson on the context of the play and people's beliefs about witches in Shakespeare's time. Write down your thoughts on how you think the audience would react to seeing three witches appear on stage.

5 Now use your notes and ideas to write an explanation of the impact of the witches on the audience. You could start your explanation like this:

> The appearance of the witches would make a great impression on the audience because...

Taking it further

1 Now look back at what the characters actually say. Reading the speeches aloud will help you here. What do you notice about the way Shakespeare has written these speeches and what effect do these language choices have?

Why do you think Shakespeare makes the witches speak in **rhyme** and in **riddles**, using **alliteration**? What could the rhyming suggest? How do you feel about someone who speaks in riddles?

2 Add your explanation of the impact and effect of the witches' language to what you have already written about the witches' appearance on the stage.

Key terms

Rhyme Words that end with the same sound.

Riddle A deliberately puzzling way of saying something.

Alliteration Words beginning with the same sound.

Check your level

LEVEL 5	I can explain the effect of Shakespeare's structural choices.
LEVEL 6	I can recognise the connotations of specific words and use this to explain their effect.
LEVEL 7	I can write a detailed analysis of Shakespeare's effects, and their effect on the audience.

Learning objective

- To consolidate and extend your analysis of Shakespeare's use of language.
- To appreciate the subtlety of Shakespeare's writing.

Bridge to GCSE

- At GCSE, you will need to develop your analysis of Shakespeare's language beyond the meaning of the individual words by making links between different characters' speeches.

Shakespeare cleverly keeps the audience in suspense – the witches mention Macbeth in the opening scene to intrigue the audience, then in the second scene we hear impressive reports of Macbeth's courage in battle. It is not until the third scene that the audience see Macbeth and begin to form their own view of him.

Getting you thinking

An injured sergeant tells Duncan, the King of Scotland, how Macbeth has performed in battle. Shakespeare introduces the sergeant as 'a good and hardy soldier' to prove to the audience he is a reliable witness.

SERGEANT	but all's too weak: For brave Macbeth – well he deserves that name – Disdaining fortune, with his brandish'd steel, Which smoked with bloody execution, Like valour's minion carved out his passage Till he faced the slave; Which ne'er shook hands, nor bade farewell to him, Till he unseam'd him from the nave to the chaps, And fix'd his head upon our battlements.
DUNCAN	O valiant cousin! worthy gentleman!

- Write down as many points as you can about Macbeth from this speech. Support each point you make with a quotation.

GCSE skills focus

The sergeant reports that Macbeth defeated the rebel Macdonwald's army, but just at their moment of victory, when they were exhausted, the King of Norway chose to attack Scotland. Duncan worries that this might have dismayed Macbeth and his friend Banquo.

SERGEANT	But the Norweyan lord surveying vantage, With furbish'd arms and new supplies of men Began a fresh assault.
DUNCAN	Dismay'd not this Our captains, Macbeth and Banquo?
SERGEANT	Yes; As sparrows eagles, or the hare the lion.

Shakespeare uses metaphors of an eagle and a 'lion' to describe Macbeth. Look at these two student comments about this line.

> The sergeant describes Macbeth and Banquo as being like 'eagles' or like 'the lion'. He uses the 'sparrows' and 'the hare' as images for the King of Norway. Macbeth and Banquo aren't dismayed or upset by the King of Norway because a lion would not be upset by a hare.

This is a very basic comment because the student has just rewritten the line, retelling what happens. Because the student hasn't really used his or her own words, it is difficult to see how well the student understands the meaning.

> Shakespeare uses images of strong, powerful animals to describe Macbeth and Banquo, and weak, pathetic animals to describe the King of Norway. The 'lion' is known as the king of beasts because he is at the top of the food chain and all the other animals are afraid of the lion, especially an animal like a 'hare' which could be seen as prey. Similarly, an eagle is one of the biggest birds in the sky and 'sparrows' are very small, so this makes the King of Norway seem insignificant in comparison with Macbeth and Banquo. Shakespeare uses 'eagles' and 'the lion' to emphasise their courage and fighting spirit against the timid 'hare' and 'sparrows'.

This is a very effective analysis, which focuses on what the writer is doing, rather than on what happens. The student has thought carefully about the connotations of the images – 'strong, powerful', 'king of beasts', 'top of the food chain'. The student makes detailed comments about the images, which show a thorough and thoughtful analysis. The comments are all linked to what the images reveal about Macbeth's character, so it is clear the student knows why Shakespeare has chosen these words.

Now you try it

Macbeth finally appears in the third scene: he is returning, victorious, from the battle, with his best friend Banquo, when they come across the three witches.

Here is Banquo's description of the witches. What is his opinion of them?

Enter Macbeth and Banquo

MACBETH	So foul and fair a day I have not seen.
BANQUO	How far is't call'd to Forres? What are these
	So wither'd and so wild in their attire,
	That look not like the inhabitants o' the earth,
	And yet are on't? Live you? or are you aught
	That man may question? You seem to understand me,
	By each at once her chappy finger laying
	Upon her skinny lips: you should be women,
	And yet your beards forbid me to interpret
	That you are so.
MACBETH	Speak, if you can: what are you?
FIRST WITCH	All hail, Macbeth! hail to thee, thane of Glamis!
SECOND WITCH	All hail, Macbeth! hail to thee, thane of Cawdor!
THIRD WITCH	All hail, Macbeth, thou shalt be king hereafter!

1 Work with your partner to discuss:
- how Banquo describes the witches
- what you think is going through Banquo's mind at this point
- why Shakespeare uses these techniques in the speech – alliteration, questions and contradictions (for example, the witches don't look like they belong on earth, but are on it).

2 Answer this question analysing the effect of Banquo's speech:

How does Shakespeare use language to create a vivid picture of the witches and reveal Banquo's thoughts about them?

Your answer should be as detailed as possible and include
- quotations
- references to the techniques Shakespeare is using
- explanations of the effect of the techniques
- your ideas about Banquo's thoughts and feelings, and why you have come to these conclusions.

These are some sentence starters you could use:
- Banquo's reaction to the witches is...
- He thinks they are...
- Shakespeare uses... to show...
- The alliteration emphasises...
- There are lots of questions in the speech, which imply...
- It is clear to the audience that...

Taking it further

After Banquo has seen the witches, Shakespeare gives us Macbeth's reaction to the witches: 'Speak if you can: what are you?' This is very different to Banquo's and is clearly a deliberate **contrast**.

Think about how Macbeth's reaction to the witches is different to Banquo's reaction, and what this suggests about Macbeth's character.

Key terms

Contrast Two opposing views placed next to each other so the reader can compare them.

1 Read Banquo's speech again and compare it with Macbeth's lines. Write a list of all the differences (or contrasts) you can identify between the two speeches.

2 Look at each difference with your partner and discuss what each one tells you about Macbeth and his thoughts and feelings towards the witches.

What have you learnt?

Write your analysis of the contrast between Banquo and Macbeth, focusing on what the scene tells us about Macbeth's thoughts and feelings.

Checklist for success

✓ Use quotations.
✓ Provide detailed discussion of language techniques and the effect they have on the audience.
✓ Include exploration of the character's thoughts and feelings.

Check your level

LEVEL 5 I can comment on the effect of words.

LEVEL 6 I can make connections between a character's language and their thoughts and feelings.

LEVEL 7 I can recognise links between language, sentence structure and the character's thoughts and feelings.

Learning objective

- To read the characters' words closely and use your imagination to empathise with their situation.

Bridge to GCSE

- At GCSE, you can apply the skills you are developing to any text. This should build your confidence when you are reading.

The play *Hamlet* begins with two soldiers having a conversation. In Shakespeare's time there was no electricity, which meant that plays were performed in the afternoon so that people could see the actors. There were simple props, but Shakespeare had to set the scene through words. In many ways the plays were more like a modern radio play, with the words giving much of the information to the listener rather than elaborate sets and scene changes.

Getting you thinking

1 In small groups, read the first 15 lines of the play below. Two people should read aloud and the others should see what information they can pick up. You should be able to find out:

- when the scene is taking place
- what the weather is like
- who the characters are, and what they are doing.

2 Once you have established the facts, discuss the thoughts and feelings of Bernardo and Francisco. Aim to be as precise as possible. Try continuing their conversation to explore what might be going on in their heads.

 **Bridge to GCSE**

Your view of the characters' thoughts and feelings, coupled with why they feel like this, is your interpretation of the character. Developing your own **interpretation** is a key GCSE skill.

Act 1, Scene 1 *Elsinore. A platform before the castle.*
Francisco at his post. Enter to him Bernardo

BERNARDO Who's there?

FRANCISO Nay, answer me: stand, and unfold yourself.

BERNARDO Long live the king!

FRANCISO Bernardo?

BERNARDO He.

FRANCISO You come most carefully upon your hour.

BERNARDO Tis now struck twelve; get thee to bed, Francisco.

FRANCISO For this relief much thanks: 'tis bitter cold,
And I am sick at heart.

BERNARDO Have you had quiet guard?

FRANCISO Not a mouse stirring.

BERNARDO Well, good night.
If you do meet Horatio and Marcellus,
The rivals of my watch, bid them make haste.

FRANCISO I think I hear them. Stand, ho! Who's there?

Enter Horatio and Marcellus

GCSE skills focus

Analysis is an important GCSE skill. Here it means **interpreting** the characters' thoughts and **explaining** how you have reached your conclusions using evidence from the text.

In a performance, the actor gives the audience an interpretation of the character through the delivery of Shakespeare's words and through actions. When you read a play, you need to be able to explain your own interpretation – this means deciding what Shakespeare wanted to suggest about the character from the words he gives to them.

Now you try it

How did you come to your conclusions about Bernardo and Francisco?

Look at the very first speech:

> BERNARDO   Who's there?

Why does Shakespeare choose to start the play with a question? Think about the atmosphere Shakespeare wants to create and decide what the best explanation is.

Explain the conclusions you reach. You could begin like this:

> Shakespeare starts the play with Bernardo asking a question, 'Who's there?' to suggest...

Taking it further

What other questions do you notice in the passage? What is their effect?

Check your level		
	LEVEL 4	I can identify key features of the scene.
	LEVEL 5	I can describe and explain the characters' thoughts and feelings.
	LEVEL 6	I can discuss how Shakespeare develops the atmosphere in the scene.

The ghost in *Hamlet*

Learning objective

● To extend analysis of Shakespeare's language.

Bridge to GCSE

● At GCSE you will develop detailed and precise comments on the use and effect of language.

In the first scene of *Hamlet*, the ghost of Hamlet's father appears to Horatio, Bernardo and Marcellus. The ghost is silent: he will only speak to his son. He does, however, make a huge impact on the characters and the audience.

Getting you thinking

Read the extract below. The guards have asked Hamlet's best friend, Horatio, to observe the ghost to get his advice.

BERNARDO	Welcome, Horatio: welcome, good Marcellus.
MARCELLUS	What, has this thing appear'd again to-night?
BERNARDO	I have seen nothing.
MARCELLUS	Horatio says 'tis but our fantasy,
	And will not let belief take hold of him
	Touching this dreaded sight, twice seen of us:
	Therefore I have entreated him along
	With us to watch the minutes of this night;
	That if again this **apparition** come,
	He may approve our eyes and speak to it.
HORATIO	Tush, tush, 'twill not appear. …
Enter Ghost	
MARCELLUS	Peace, break thee off; look, where it comes again!
BERNARDO	In the same figure, like the king that's dead.
MARCELLUS	Thou art a scholar; speak to it, Horatio.
BERNARDO	Looks it not like the king? Mark it, Horatio.
HORATIO	Most like: it **harrows** me with fear and wonder.
BERNARDO	It would be spoke to.
MARCELLUS	Question it, Horatio.
HORATIO	What art thou that **usurp'st** this time of night,
	Together with that fair and warlike form
	In which the majesty of buried Denmark
	Did sometimes march? By heaven I charge thee, speak!
MARCELLUS	It is offended.
BERNARDO	See, it stalks away!
HORATIO	Stay! speak, speak! I charge thee, speak!
Exit Ghost	
MARCELLUS	'Tis gone, and will not answer.
BERNARDO	How now, Horatio! you tremble and look pale:
	Is not this something more than fantasy?
	What think you on't?
HORATIO	Before my God, I might not this believe
	Without the sensible and true **avouch**
	Of mine own eyes.

Glossary

apparition Ghostly figure.

harrows To harrow means to distress or vex. Horatio is saying that seeing the king's ghost is shocking and disturbing.

usurp'st Usurp means to take over without authority. In other words, the ghost has no right to be there.

avouch Guarantee

With a partner, discuss the effect of the ghost being silent.
- What do you think is going through the minds of the characters?
- What questions do you think the audience might be asking themselves?

GCSE skills focus

Shakespeare uses language and structure very carefully here for many subtle effects. Noticing little things about language will help you to interpret the scene. You might write, for example:

> The way Bernardo questions Horatio after the ghost's appearance, 'Is not this something more than fantasy?', suggests he is pleased to be been proved right. Earlier Horatio doubted what the guards have seen, calling it a 'fantasy', so Bernardo sarcastically throws his word back at hime, and enjoys questioning Horatio in return. Horatio has been convinced by what he has seen and this would help to convince the audience that the ghost is real.

Now you try it

With your partner, discuss the following features of the scene:
- having the characters talk about the ghost before the ghost actually appears
- the different words used at first to refer to the ghost, and then the repeated use of the pronoun 'it' to refer to the ghost once it appears – what do these tell you about their attitudes to the ghost?
- the punctuation, repetition and short sentences when Horatio tries to command the ghost in the line, 'Stay! speak, speak! I charge thee, speak!'

In each case, decide what the language reveals about the characters' thoughts and feelings.

What have you learnt?

Share the conclusions you have drawn about one of these features of the scene with the rest of the class.

Check your level

LEVEL 6	I can comment on aspects of language and their effect.
LEVEL 7	I can appreciate how language is used to develop characters and atmosphere.
LEVEL 8	I can show my engagement with the text by developing my own interpretations.

Your Bridge to GCSE task

Learning objective

- To consider how to plan and organise ideas effectively.

Bridge to GCSE

- At GCSE you will learn to structure your written response to show your understanding of a text.

In this lesson you will see how careful planning and organisation is an essential part of writing clearly and confidently about texts.

GCSE skills focus

Planning is the secret of clear and effective writing. Time invested in planning properly and carefully will help you to show your understanding of the plays, will make writing easier, and will be repaid in terms of better results.

There are two main elements to planning – gathering ideas and then organising those ideas. You have already spent a long time thinking about the plays, so you should have plenty of ideas. Now you need to organise your ideas well to show your understanding.

Imagine you want to open a supermarket. You decide not to buy shelves, so that you can sell everything a little more cheaply. You know what you want to sell, so you get hold of everything and make a big pile of it in the middle of the floor. Next door, another supermarket opens. It is a bit more expensive to buy food there, but everything is clearly organised and easy to find on shelves. Where do you think most people will choose to shop?

- Try to think of other situations where planning and structure makes things work more efficiently. Share your examples.

Bridge to GCSE

In your GCSE course you will be given a guideline word limit and a specific amount of time in which to complete your work.

Your task

Read the task below carefully and highlight the key words. Make sure you are completely clear about what you are being asked to do.

> *Compare how Shakespeare creates atmosphere in the opening scenes of* **Macbeth** *and* **Hamlet***.*

The question asks you to do a number of things. You will need to

- compare two plays
- explain how Shakespeare does things
- focus on the atmosphere in the plays.

Bridge to GCSE

Effective writing always focuses on what the writer does, not on what happens in the play. Using Shakespeare's name at the start of sentences makes you focus on the writer and shows you are addressing the question.

Plan your response

There is no single right way of planning – you can have a brilliant idea for your essay at any point. A good place to start is by jotting down all the things you know about the main focus of the essay – the supernatural. A mind map, like the one below, can be very useful.

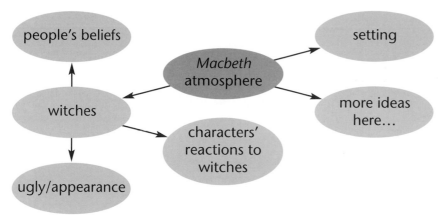

people's beliefs

setting

Macbeth atmosphere

witches

more ideas here...

characters' reactions to witches

ugly/appearance

1 Look back through the scenes you have read and the notes you have made. Try to include as many ideas as you can in your mind map.

2 Find quotations from both *Macbeth* and *Hamlet* that support the ideas in your mind map. For example, you could say that the witches are ugly and unpleasant to look at, using supporting evidence from Banquo's description of them having 'skinny lips' and 'beards'.

Top tip

It is essential that you discuss how Shakespeare uses language and dramatic devices in the play. To do this you will need to find quotations and examples. Choose quotations that you are confident with and will be able to discuss in lots of detail.

4 Another way in which you can show your understanding of the plays is to make links and comparisons between them. These can be similarities or differences and should include dramatic devices and imagery. Think about the two plays and make as many connections as you can between them.

Macbeth	Hamlet
• Supernatural – witches • Characters unsure about what the witches are – Banquo says, 'That look not like the inhabitants of the earth' • The witches speak	• Supernatural – ghost • Characters unsure about what they are seeing – refer to ghost as 'it', 'thing' • At first the ghost is silent

If you have made a lot of connections, you could identify the five most interesting ones to use later on. A good essay does not have to cover absolutely everything: it is much better to show a really detailed understanding of a few aspects of the plays.

5 Have a **big idea**. To write a really effective essay you need to come up with a **big idea** that glues all your smaller points together.

- Your **big idea** could be a bold statement about the plays, which you are going to go on and prove by analysing the texts.

- The question is an invitation to you to explain your own opinions and ideas – your interpretation of the plays.

- Like all GCSE exam questions and controlled assessment tasks, the essay question is open-ended. It gives you a big topic to discuss – the atmosphere – and is encouraging you to give your own interpretation.

6 Write down a sentence about the atmosphere at the start of the plays. Try to choose two or three descriptive words. Now write down why you think Shakespeare wanted the atmosphere to be like this. There are various possible reasons – say what you think.

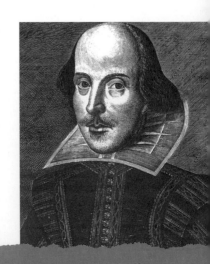

These two statements are conclusions you have reached from studying the play – they are your **big idea**, which you can use to hold together all the bits of knowledge, information and understanding you have about the plays.

Write your response

You have gathered lots of ideas about the play. This is the first part of planning.

The next thing is to organise those ideas. You need to select the ones that will support your **big idea** and put them into a sensible order. Use the framework below to help you complete the second stage of your planning.

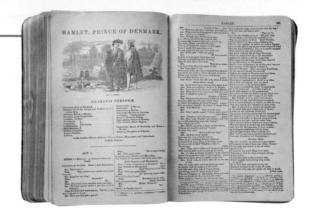

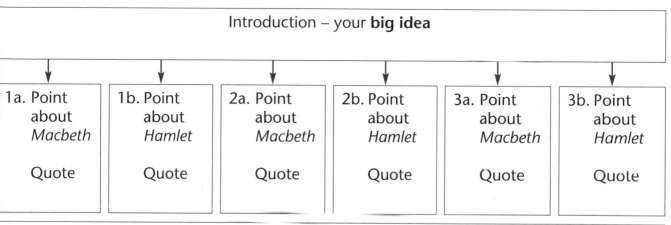

Introduction – your **big idea**

| 1a. Point about *Macbeth* Quote | 1b. Point about *Hamlet* Quote | 2a. Point about *Macbeth* Quote | 2b. Point about *Hamlet* Quote | 3a. Point about *Macbeth* Quote | 3b. Point about *Hamlet* Quote |

Conclusion – perhaps something about the similarities or differences between the two plays

Each box connected to your **big idea** will become a detailed paragraph in your essay, in which you will explain carefully how some aspect of the play works. You can, of course, have more than six paragraphs in your essay.

Bridge to GCSE

Moving backwards and forwards between the two plays is better than writing about one play and then about the other, as it shows you are making links and connections and highlights your understanding of the texts.

Checklist for success

✔ Use planning techniques such as mind maps, spider diagrams and frameworks to help you organise your ideas and present them in a logical order.

✔ Find quotations to support the points you make.

✔ Make links and comparisons between the two plays.

✔ Have a **big idea** that connects all the points you want to make in your essay.

Learning objective

- To learn techniques and skills for sophisticated essay writing.

Bridge to GCSE

- At GCSE you will develop an appropriate writing style to demonstrate your appreciation and analysis of texts.

Part of reviewing your work involves seeing where you can make improvements to the way you write as well as to the ideas you have presented.

There are some techniques that you can use to show you are an accomplished and confident writer.

Read these two examples of students' work about Shakespeare's use of the weather at the start of the plays.

Dawn's answer

At the start of <u>Macbeth</u> the weather is very bad, there is 'Thunder and lightning' which is scary weather and might make people jump. The witches also talk about the weather when they say 'Hover through the fog and filthy air.' which suggests a misty, gloomy atmosphere. I think this is the sort of weather witches would like because they could hide in it and do evil things.

At the start of <u>Hamlet</u> it is the middle of the night and the weather is very cold. One of the guards, Francisco, says 'I am sick at heart', which shows that he is fed up and doesn't want to be on guard any more. I think this is a dark and nasty time of night which is just the sort of time that a ghost would appear.

Examiner comment:

Dawn is tending to describe what happens in the play. She is using quotations to support her points and is beginning to make comments on the weather, but these are quite simple and undeveloped. This would be a good Level 4, which could move up towards a Level 5 with more careful explanation of how the text works.

Darryl's answer

Shakespeare begins <u>Macbeth</u> with 'Thunder and lightning' which is very powerful, dramatic weather that would immediately grab the audience's attention and get them interested in what is happening on the stage. The witches' reference to the 'fog and filthy air' reinforces the sense of the weather being used as a signal for bad things happening.

Similarly, <u>Hamlet</u> also uses cold weather along with the middle of the night to build tension in the play. Shakespeare shows that the characters are nervous and on edge: Francisco says he is 'sick at heart' because of the cold, but his unhappiness at the cold, dark situation is also preparing the audience for the appearance of the ghost.

Examiner comment:

In this extract Darryl focuses on what the writer is doing (not what happens in the play) and explains the effect of the writer's choices, developing his ideas with detailed comments. Darryl supports his comments with short, precise quotations and makes a connection between the two plays. This short extract would suggest a strong Level 6.

Here are four things you can do to write more effectively:

1 Use the writer's name. Starting sentences with Shakespeare's name makes you write about his techniques, rather than what happens in the play or what the characters are doing.

2 Use short, **embedded quotations** to show you are focusing on specific words, not just copying out great chunks of the play.

3 Use words like *similarly, also, likewise, in contrast, however* that show you are comparing the two texts.

4 Avoid using the first person *'I think...'* Your essay is all your ideas, so you don't need to use this.

Key terms

Embedded quotation The quotation forms a natural part of the sentence.

Top tip

Quotation marks are used to show when you are using someone else's words. You should never write *I quote* in your essay – this is repetitive, unnecessary and unhelpful.

Check your progress

In this chapter you have looked at parts of two Shakespearean plays. You should have begun to develop your own ideas about the characters and themes of the plays and be able to explain how you have reached these conclusions.

Taking it further

Read the lists in the boxes below. Which Level do you think you have reached in this chapter, and what do you need to do to improve?

LEVEL 5 (Aiming for GCSE C/B)

AF2 I can identify the main points and support them with quotations.

AF3 I can explain the ideas and meaning of texts.

AF4 I can comment on structure showing some awareness of the writer's intentions.

AF5 I can identify various features of language use with some comment on effects.

AF6 I can explain how the context of the text relates to its meaning.

LEVEL 6 (Aiming for GCSE B/A)

AF2 I can identify relevant points and support them with apt quotations.

AF3 I can explore the themes and ideas of texts in detail.

AF4 I can discuss how structural choices support the writer's ideas.

AF5 I can explain in detail how language is used and its effect on the reader.

AF6 I can discuss how the context of a text affects its meaning.

LEVEL 7 (Aiming for GCSE A/A*)

AF2 I can illustrate my interpretation of texts with precise selection of quotations and references.

AF3 I can begin to show insightful interpretation of texts, making connections between ideas.

AF4 I can evaluate the effect of the writer's structural choices.

AF5 I can analyse language use perceptively with appreciation of its effects.

AF6 I can analyse how meaning and interpretation relate to the context of the text.

Next steps to GCSE

At GCSE you will be expected to read at least one Shakespeare play. You may be asked to compare it with another Shakespeare play or a different text with a similar theme. You will also be expected to write about other literary texts, which may include novels, plays, short stories and poems.

Chapter 5

Reading non-fiction texts

In this chapter you will learn how to analyse non-fiction texts, focusing on how writers present ideas and on how to follow an argument through a text. The non-fiction texts you will read and write about have a shared theme of health and body image.

Bridge to GCSE

To get you ready for your GCSE course, this chapter will take you through the following steps:

Explore ideas ❯
- Develop active reading strategies.
- Analyse and comment on how a text has been written and structured.

Check your skills ❯
- Learn how to analyse the way writers use language, structure and presentational features.

Extend your skills ❯
- Learn how to develop effective comparisons between texts.

Plan and write ❯
- Plan and write a comparison of two texts under timed conditions.

Improve your work ❯
- Review your response and set yourself a target for improvement.

Your GCSE-style assessment task will be to compare two non-fiction texts.

Key Stage 3 Reading Assessment Focuses		GCSE English/English Language Reading Assessment Objectives	
AF2	Understand, describe, select or retrieve information, events or ideas from texts and use quotation and reference to text	AO2/3i	Read and understand texts, selecting material appropriate to purpose, collating from different sources and making comparisons and cross-references as appropriate
AF4	Identify and comment on the structure and organisation of texts, including grammatical and presentational features at text level	AO2/3iii	Explain and evaluate how writers use linguistic, grammatical, structural and presentational features to achieve effects and engage and influence the reader
AF5	Explain and comment on writers' use of language, including grammatical and literary features at word and sentence level		

What is a non-fiction text?

A non-fiction text is any text that focuses on fact rather than fiction. When we read non-fiction we expect the 'facts' to be true. When we read fiction or watch a film or play we don't expect everything to be true – we understand that the author is telling a story. Fiction texts (stories, novels and plays) usually have one main purpose: to entertain.

Most non-fiction texts have a clear form and audience, and the writer has a definite purpose.

Getting you thinking

You have already written hundreds of non-fiction texts, from emails to text messages to essays for school. You also read them all the time – in fact, we are all bombarded with non-fiction texts everywhere we look.

Without realising it you are probably already quite expert at identifying the FAP (**F**orm, **A**udience, **P**urpose) of non-fiction texts. Even the back of your cereal box has a clear form, audience and purpose.

1 Working with a partner, see how many different forms of non-fiction text you can think of. You could use the following prompts to get your list started:

● items that come through your letterbox
● what you see as you walk around a supermarket
● how you find out about a famous person's life
● what you see on a newsagent's shelves
● instructions in a food technology lesson.

2 Take one of the non-fiction forms you and your partner have written down. Describe it to your class without using its name. Can they guess what the form is? For example:

● comes through the door with the mail
● is usually asking you to do something
● is folded over
● often uses pictures, colour or photographs
● is inserted into magazines.

Answer: Leaflet

GCSE skills focus

Sometimes non-fiction texts have a clear and specific target audience: for example, cookery enthusiasts or video game players. Often, however, the audience is more general and harder to pin down. For example, think about a TV listings magazine: it would be quite difficult to describe the audience, because it is so general and includes many different types of people.

The intended audience for the text influences the style, language and presentational features used to achieve the purpose. The audience might have certain things in common, for example:

- age range
- gender
- interests and hobbies
- political beliefs
- social status.

Think of some other things that an audience for a text might share.

Now you try it

1 Look at this list of non-fiction texts. Discuss with a partner which ones are written for a general audience and which are written for a specific target audience:

- advice sheet on how to potty-train a toddler
- leaflet on energy-saving hints included with an electricity bill
- magazine for model railway enthusiasts
- news report in a daily broadsheet newspaper
- billboard advertisement for a luxury car
- poster advertising a nu-metal rock concert.

2 What might you be able to assume about the age, gender and family circumstances of these target audiences?

Taking it further

1 Look at the three non-fiction texts below. For each one, identify

- the form
- the audience
- the purpose.

2 Now see if you can identify three key features (conventions) of the form.

For each feature, write a sentence that includes a short piece of evidence (quotation) to highlight what the feature is. So, for example, you might begin with:

> Source 1 is a… It can be identified as this form of text because of the type of sentences that are used, for example: '…' Also, the sentences follow a sequence which suggests that…'

Bridge to GCSE

At GCSE you will be expected to comment on how language and presentational features are used to influence the reader. Think about how writers adapt their sentence structure and vocabulary as well as the content of their writing to suit their **form**, **audience** and **purpose**.

3 Think about the similarities and differences between the texts. Work with a partner and each choose two of the three texts. (Don't pick the same two.) Allow yourselves five minutes to explain to each other:

- the strongest similarity between your two texts
- the biggest difference between your two texts.

Source 1

Gooey chocolate cake

Heat the oven to 190 degrees C.

Grease and line two 20 cm baking tins.

- First melt the chocolate in a heat-proof bowl.
- Beat the butter and sugar until light and fluffy.
- Add the cooled melted chocolate and stir well.
- Next, fold in the flour and baking powder.
- Spoon the mixture into the prepared baking tins.
- Bake for 25 minutes or until top is springy.

Source 2

Source 3

? problem page

Q I've got 3 sons, and the smallest one just wants to copy his older brothers all the time – especially when it comes to mealtimes! He can't understand why he has to have a smaller portion. What can I do?

A The first thing to do is to explain about how bodies of different ages are different sizes, and to get him to look at the difference in the size of his fist compared with his brothers. The hand drawing activity in the Kids' Stuff section will be useful for this. You can also get him to look at the diagram on page 7 – maybe read it with him and explain what too much food can do. It might also be helpful to make him Head of Portion Police and make it his job to dish up everyone's dinner and work out how much they need so he feels involved in the decision.

Bridge to GCSE

Become experts at finding the FAP whenever you look at a non-fiction text. It should be the first thing you determine when you approach a new text for the first time.

What have you learnt?

You have been learning how to identify the **form, audience** and **purpose** (FAP) of a non-fiction text. You have also started to think about some of the conventions of non-fiction texts and consider the similarities and differences between two different texts.

Check your level

LEVEL 5	I can identify most relevant points and support them with appropriate quotation.
LEVEL 6	I can easily identify relevant points and use well-chosen, appropriate quotation.
LEVEL 7	I can precisely identify relevant points and make close analytical reference to the text.

One of the most important lessons you can learn about GCSE English is that most of the skills are 'transferable'. This means that you use similar techniques and skills when you read and respond to poetry or Shakespeare or a novel or, in this case, non-fiction texts.

Getting you thinking

Some texts present a particular viewpoint very clearly and use particular techniques to persuade the reader that this viewpoint is right. These types of text are presenting an argument – a considered, developed point of view.

Read Source 4, below, from the introduction to *The First-time Cook* by Sophie Grigson.

Source 4

Why cook?

Good question. Why should you learn to cook at all? You'll get by just fine on takeaways, ready-meals, sandwiches, crisps and chocolate. Nobody needs to cook at all these days, as long as they own a microwave, a kettle and a toaster.

This is potentially a good thing, and certainly hugely liberating. Before you throw the book down in disgust, let me explain. Cooking should be and can be a thoroughly enjoyable, life-enhancing task. There is such pleasure to be had from working with beautiful, fresh, natural produce, […] from combining ingredients to expose their finest most enticing flavours […]. All this before you even get to the climax of the whole endeavour – the eating itself.

How miserable then, when cooking becomes a tyranny, which it can when there is a day-in-day-out obligation to put a proper cooked meal on the table. So to me, the ideal is a balanced compromise between real cooking as often as possible, and convenience food as back-up for those days when work or play has sapped your energy. There's nothing wrong with beans on toast every now and then.

1 Discuss with a partner:

- What is the FAP of this text? How do you know?

- What is Grigson's overall argument?

2 Now, let's start thinking about how the writer achieves her purpose. See if you can answer these questions about various features of the text:

- What does Grigson appear to be saying in the first paragraph of the text?

- Does Grigson consider an alternative point of view, or just present her own opinion?

- Can you spot the **topic sentences** she uses to develop her ideas?

- Is the tone **formal** or **informal**? Is there any humour?

- Is the vocabulary formal or are there **colloquialisms**?

- Is there any emotive or descriptive vocabulary?

- Do you notice any hyperbole (exaggeration for effect)?

Key terms

Topic sentences Introduce or sum up the topic of the paragraph.

Formal Distant and reserved, with clear rules on what is appropriate.

Informal Relaxed, friendly, with less emphasis on rules.

Colloquialism Word or phrase used in everyday, conversational language. Can include 'slang' terms.

Bridge to GCSE

Comment, don't describe. Short, embedded quotations make you sound focused and purposeful because you are using the text to illustrate your points and ideas.

GCSE skills focus

Being able to comment on a text, rather than describe or recount what it says, is a very important skill.

Commenting on a text means thinking about **how** it has been written rather than simply what it is about. Commenting means considering how the text works: considering the techniques used and – very importantly – the **purpose** and **effect** of those techniques.

Using evidence in the form of short, precise quotations is really important here.

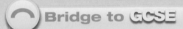 **Bridge to GCSE**

Examiners often say that the depth of a student's comment is the key difference between an E grade and a C grade at GCSE. Grade C work focuses on **how** the text is written rather than what it is about.

Now you try it

Look at this example of student work:

> Sophie is arguing that learning to cook is a really good idea. I know this because she says:
>
> 'Cooking should be and can be a thoroughly enjoyable, life-enhancing task. There is such pleasure to be had from working with beautiful, fresh, natural produce, from combining ingredients to expose their finest most enticing flavours, a kind of magic that is there to be discovered by every person who walks into a kitchen with appetite and hunger.'
>
> This shows that she thinks learning to cook is really fun and enjoyable.

Makes a clear point but needs to use writer's second name

Try: 'she suggests' or 'this is highlighted by' instead

This is a very long quotation; using a shorter quotation would show that the student is focusing on precise detail

This isn't a comment, it's a paraphrase (repetition in your own words) of the quotation

Now read the student's revised piece of work:

Grigson is arguing that learning to cook is really enjoyable. She uses emotive vocabulary such as 'life-enhancing' to suggest that the process will improve your life as well as what you eat. This is supported with powerful, positive vocabulary such as 'beautiful fresh produce' and 'enticing flavours' to reinforce her message. The phrase 'kind of magic' suggests that a cook is like a magician in the kitchen, exposing all the real wonders of food with their skill. This is very persuasive as an argument as it seems to suggest the power that a good cook can possess as well as the fun and satisfaction that can be gained from the process. Grigson uses language to infect the reader with her enthusiasm and confidence.

- Uses the writer's last name – this sounds much more purposeful and appropriate
- Makes a clear introductory point
- Starts to consider how the point is being made by focusing on what the writer does
- Short, relevant quotation embedded into student sentence
- Starts to develop the analysis with further embedded evidence
- Really starting to analyse language effects here by considering the effect of the 'magic' analogy
- Two clear comments on how the language affects the reader

● Write down three improvements that the student has made.

What have you learnt?

Sentences **a** to **c** below are quite basic. Rewrite the sentences using the skills in the Top tip box:

a Sophie uses lots of words that make her tone sound friendly and chatty.

b The text makes it seem as if the writer doesn't think cooking is a good idea at the start, but she does this for effect.

c The writer makes it seem really easy to learn how to cook so that it is not threatening.

Top tip

- Identify a specific technique used by the writer.
- Comment on the reason for that technique being used.
- Use some short evidence to support your point.

Check your level

LEVEL 5 I can identify most relevant points and support them with appropriate quotation.

LEVEL 6 I can easily identify relevant points and use well-chosen, appropriate quotation.

LEVEL 7 I can precisely identify relevant points and make close analytical reference to the text.

- To analyse how a writer has used structure and organisation to develop his or her argument.

Bridge to GCSE

- At GCSE, you will need to recognise the writer's viewpoint and focus on some of the ways writers present their viewpoint to the reader.

There are many ways in which writers communicate their ideas and points of view. As well as language techniques, the structure and organisation of ideas are important to consider. When reading texts that argue a particular 'case' or point of view, being able to trace this argument through the structure of the writing is vital. When you start noticing and identifying features of structure and organisation, your own writing often improves as well – an added bonus for GCSE.

Getting you thinking

Read Source 5, an article by Lucy Mangan from the *Telegraph* newspaper.

Source 5

Before and after: an old-fashioned kind of advertising scandal

Johnson & Johnson has had an ad banned for being misleading.
But other advertising scandals have been much more serious.

The road to hell is paved with good intentions and a light dusting of face powder. This should be the lesson learned by Johnson & Johnson this week, after an advert for their Clean & Clear acne kit was banned by the Advertising Standards Association. It found that the use of makeup on its models created a misleading impression of the product's powers.

In the 'before' shots, the kit's users looked like normal teenagers – heaving masses of overactive sebaceous glands and eyes filled with despair. In the 'after' shots, they glowed like the morning dew and complaints were received about the disparity. Johnson & Johnson said they used only powder to prevent camera flare obscuring the 'fewer spots, reduced redness and much clearer skin'.

It seems almost unfair that the company has been chastised for what is, in this day and age, a fairly minimal intervention. Most recent cosmetic advertising scandals have required the addition of false parts (Cheryl Cole's hair extensions, Penelope Cruz's fake eyelashes) or major digital enhancement (Twiggy's peepers in a recent ad for eye cream were made to look like sapphires the size of your fist) before they registered on the public outrage-o-meter.

Plus, the before-and-after format is so endearingly old-fashioned. It recalls the Grecian 2000 ads of yesteryear or the (alas now defunct) *Innovations* catalogue. It used to sell some posture-improving item and in the 'before' shot the woman was indistinguishable from Quasimodo. Her hair hung lankly round her pallid face, the lighting was funereal and she wore a drab, high-necked top. But after? Why, after, the device had not only given her the deportment of an Edwardian duchess but rosy cheeks, a skin-tight top and a whole new lighting rig!

The format survives in the makeover stories in women's weeklies and in plastic-surgery ads in the back of other magazines. But the media now prefers to present us with airbrushed images – the unacknowledged 'after' shots. A standard of impossible perfection, after all, shifts more units than apparently attainable improvements will ever do.

1 The most important first task is to identify the FAP. What is the FAP of Source 5?

2 Topic sentences introduce the topic or subject of the paragraph and direct the overall argument of the whole text. You can think of topic sentences as serving a similar purpose to a subheading.

Take each of the five paragraphs from Source 5 in turn. For each paragraph, create a subheading that accurately sums up the main point or purpose of the paragraph.

3 What is the overall 'argument' being presented in this text? Discuss your ideas with a partner.

GCSE skills focus

An 'argument tree' is a way of organising your ideas visually (a graphic organiser). Argument trees can help you to analyse the structure and organisation of ideas in a non-fiction text.

Argument trees can look like this:

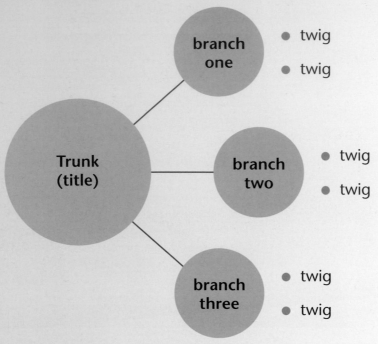

- The 'trunk' of your tree should contain the main point or title of the whole text.
- The 'branches' are the main points being made by the writer, usually divided into separate paragraphs.
- The 'twigs' are the development of each point: the evidence, the statistics, the detail used to reinforce each main point.

Bridge to GCSE

You can also use argument trees to plan your own non-fiction writing when you are asked to argue a viewpoint.

Now you try it

Read Source 5 on page 114 again.

1 Construct your own argument tree for this article. Remember to
- identify the main point in the 'trunk'
- use one 'branch' for the topic of each of the five paragraphs
- use 'twigs' to identify how each point is illustrated or developed.

What have you learnt?

Now you have analysed the structure of this text, can you comment on Lucy Mangan's viewpoint?

Even better, can you identify any language features she may be using to make her case? Can you find examples of

- sophisticated vocabulary
- use of quotations
- **rhetorical questions**
- humour
- **hyperbole**
- **emotive** or descriptive vocabulary?

What kind of tone does Lucy Mangan create in the way she uses these features?

You will look at language features in more detail later in this chapter.

 Key terms

Rhetorical questions
Questions used for effect, to which the author may then provide an answer.

Hyperbole Exaggeration for effect.

Emotive Aiming to make the reader feel an emotion.

Check your level

(LEVEL 5) I can identify the main purpose of the article with some limited explanation.

(LEVEL 6) I can identify the writer's viewpoint and provide a developed explanation with evidence.

(LEVEL 7) I can analyse the writer's viewpoint and purpose and trace the development of the argument.

Reading involves 'decoding' meaning. The words on the page are very important of course, but it is also important to consider how the text *looks* on the page.

The layout, visual appeal and organisation of a text are usually referred to as its 'presentational features'.

Getting you thinking

Presentational features include:

● pictures
● photographs
● use of colour
● images such as logos
● size and shape of font
● layout of text – headings and sub headings, columns, lists, bullet points.

Ask yourself **why** presentational features have been used. What is their purpose? What effect are they intended to have on the reader?

Advertisements are a form of non-fiction text with a clear purpose: to persuade the reader to do something (usually to buy the product). The audience will depend upon what is being advertised and where the advertisement appears.

Text-based advertisements usually contain some of the following **conventions**:

● direct address to the reader (using 'you')
● command or imperative phrases (telling you to do something)
● short simple sentences rather than long complex sentences
● powerful vocabulary for effect
● colour scheme designed to appeal to the target audience
● slogan or tag line
● logo
● use of typefaces (fonts) for effect or emphasis
● use of images.

1 Look at the two examples on the next page. Can you find any of these conventions in either advertisement?

Key terms

Conventions Types of features commonly associated with a particular form of text.

Source 6

Source 7

2 Now think about the similarities and differences.
- What is the purpose of each advertisement?
- How do you know that each item is aimed at a different target audience?
- Where would you see each item? Is there a difference in their form?

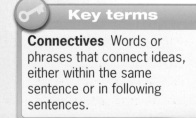

Bridge to GCSE

It is likely that one question in your GCSE examination or controlled assessment will require you to compare two items with each other.

GCSE skills focus

Source 6 is a printed advertisement, most likely to appear in a magazine; Source 7 is the front of a cereal box. However, both are advertising a product and both use presentational features to do this.

When comparing, you look for similarities and differences. If both texts were exactly the same or had nothing in common, it would be a waste of time looking for comparisons.

When you write a comparative response, try to write about both texts at the same time, comparing and contrasting as you write. Comparative vocabulary, or **connectives**, will help you to structure your response.

Similarities	Differences
Also	However
Similarly/in a similar way	On the other hand
Additionally	Conversely
Another common feature in both items	Whereas

Key terms

Connectives Words or phrases that connect ideas, either within the same sentence or in following sentences.

Now you try it

1 Look at Sources 8 and 9, two more advertisements.
Use the table below to help you start organising your ideas.

⭐ **Top tip**

Remember: identify the FAP before you do anything else.

Feature	Source 8	Source 9
Aimed at young people, particularly teenage boys		
Aimed at parents of young children		
Suggests that the product is healthy		
Addresses the reader directly		
Uses commands/imperatives		
Focuses on body image		
Uses language designed to appeal to the target audience		
Uses bright, eye-catching colours		
Uses subtle, sophisticated colours		
Uses photographs as the main focus of the text		

Source 8

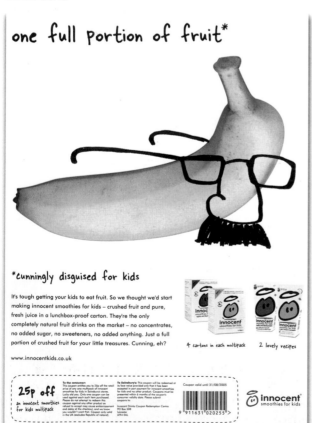

one full portion of fruit*

*cunningly disguised for kids

It's tough getting your kids to eat fruit. So we thought we'd start making innocent smoothies for kids – crushed fruit and pure, fresh juice in a lunchbox-proof carton. They're the only completely natural fruit drinks on the market – no concentrates, no added sugar, no sweeteners, no added anything. Just a full portion of crushed fruit for your little treasures. Cunning, eh?

www.innocentkids.co.uk

4 cartons in each multipack   2 lovely recipes

25p off
an innocent smoothies for kids multipack

innocent
smoothies for kids

Source 9

thedavidbeckhamacademy.com

Goal by Beckham.
Body by milk.

Heads up. The protein in milk helps build muscle and some studies suggest teens who choose it tend to be leaner. Staying active, eating right, and drinking 3 glasses a day of lowfat or fat free milk helps you look great. So grab a glass and get in the game.

got milk?

2 Now you have all your information and your list of comparative vocabulary, see if you can answer the following exam-style question:

> *Compare the way advertisers have used presentational features to appeal to their target audiences in these two texts.*

You should aim to write around 200 words. Try to complete your response in 20 minutes.

Bridge to GCSE

Getting used to working under timed conditions is excellent preparation for GCSE.

What have you learnt?

Here is how one student responded to the question above:

Both Source 8 and Source 9 are text-based adverts for food products: fruit smoothie and milk. However, whereas Source 8 is addressed to parents, Source 9 is definitely aimed at teenage boys, in particular boys who have David Beckham as a role model.

Source 8 uses a humorous graffiti-style graphic with a big photo of a banana. This eye-catching visual picks up on the 'joke' in the text about the product being 'cunningly disguised' fruit. This eye-catching image and the joke talk directly to parents by saying that the advertiser (Innocent) understands how it can be hard for parents to get their children to eat fruit. The fresh clean look of the ad, with one simple image and a lot of white space, also reflects the freshness of the product.

On the other hand, the image in Source 9 is darker and much more subdued, creating a more sophisticated and grown-up feel to the advert. This creates the impression that only sophisticated, cool people drink milk – like David Beckham. The ad encourages boys, in particular, to see themselves as potential athletes, who might hope to become as fit and 'lean' as Beckham. Unlike the first ad, which uses humour, this one uses a celebrity to get attention. He has been chosen because he is known to be fit and healthy.

- What Level would you give this response? Look at the Check your level box below and discuss with a partner what you would award this piece of writing. Then, swap your own work with your partner and award a Level to each other's work in the same way.

Check your level

LEVEL 4 I can notice some basic features of presentation and organisation.

LEVEL 5 I can identify and make comments on presentational features.

LEVEL 6 I can start to explore how presentational features are used to appeal to the audience.

Learning objective

● To analyse and compare how different writers use language and techniques to present their viewpoints.

Bridge to GCSE

● At GCSE you will have to stretch and extend your reading skills by reading longer, more challenging texts.

'Language features' can include anything the writer does with words (either vocabulary or linguistic devices) to make their point of view clear to the reader.

Humour can be used to make serious points. The two writers in this section both use irony and sarcasm to make some very strong criticisms. They also have similar points to make.

Getting you thinking

Key terms

Objective Present facts in a neutral, balanced way, not influenced by the author's personal opinions.

Some texts that are written to present an argument are careful to be **objective**. Others may be less so.

Read Source 10, an extract from *The Road to Wigan Pier* by the celebrated writer and essayist, George Orwell. It describes the time he spent in the north of England in the 1930s, living with and getting to understand the lives of working people there.

1 As you are reading the extract, think about the following questions:
  ● What is the mood or tone of this text?
  ● What is Orwell's main point in this text?

Source 10

The miner's family spend only tenpence a week on green vegetables and tenpence halfpenny on milk (remember that one of them is a child less than three years old), and nothing on fruit; but they spend one and nine on sugar (about eight pounds of sugar, that is) and a shilling on tea. [...] Would it not be better if they spent more money on wholesome things like oranges and wholemeal bread or if they even [...] saved on fuel and ate their carrots raw? Yes, it would, but the point is that no ordinary human being is ever going to do such a thing. The ordinary human being would rather starve than live on brown bread and raw carrots. And the peculiar evil is this, that the less money you have, the less inclined you feel to spend it on wholesome food.

A millionaire may enjoy breakfasting off orange juice and Ryvita biscuits; an unemployed man doesn't. [...] When you are unemployed, which is to say when you are underfed, harassed, bored, and miserable, you don't *want* to eat dull, wholesome food. You want something a bit 'tasty'. [...] White bread-and-marg and sugared tea don't nourish you to any extent, but they are nicer (at least most people think so) than brown bread-and-dripping and cold water.

Unemployment is a misery that has got to be constantly **palliated**, and especially with tea, the Englishman's opium. A cup of tea or even an aspirin is much better as a temporary **stimulant** than a crust of brown bread.

Glossary

Palliated Made less unpleasant.

Stimulant Substance used to heighten senses or increase energy.

2 Read Source 10 again, and see if you can identify examples of the following language features, thinking in each case about their effect:

- comparisons
- rhetorical questions which are then answered by the writer
- the use of lists
- irony/sarcasm (saying something different from what you mean, for effect)
- hyperbole (exaggeration for effect)
- emotive language (language intended to work on the reader's feelings)
- facts or figures
- punctuation for effect
- colloquial style.

Bridge to GCSE

Think about the term 'bias' as you read this extract. Is Orwell presenting a balanced viewpoint or is it biased? Could he be presenting a stereotyped view?

GCSE skills focus

Humour can make a powerful point, especially when the writer uses irony or sarcasm as a way of making fun of the opposing argument.

Irony can be described as a 'gap' or 'distance' between what is said and what is meant. When this is exaggerated and meant to make a cutting point, it is described as sarcasm.

Humour can also be created through mockery, imitation and hyperbole (exaggeration).

Now you try it

Now read Source 11, an article by Charlie Brooker, from *The Guardian*, Friday 6 October 2006.

Source 11

Supposing ... You are not what you eat

On a street near my home there's a gigantic poster, depicting a grisly photograph of a young girl glugging a five-litre bottle of cooking oil. The oil is pouring down her chin and over her shirt. It looks disgusting and is designed to put you off eating crisps. 'What goes into crisps goes into you,' shrieks the tagline. Do you see? […]

What their stupid poster is trying to say is this: if you eat a large bag of crisps every day for a year, you're effectively 'drinking' almost five litres of cooking oil. But so what? Drinking five litres of cooking oil would indeed be awful, but only if you necked it in one go. Sip it in tiny quantities over a full year and it might be quite pleasant. Or you could drizzle it over some crisps. That'd be even nicer. […]

St Jamie Oliver pulled the same stunt on his recent *Return to School Dinners*,

mixing chips and cakes and fat into an almighty steaming lump in front of horrified onlookers. As a spectacle, it's stomach churning; as dietary advice, it's meaningless. Churn a ton of pesto, scallops, muesli and yoghurt together and it'll look just as grim. […] Still, who cares if the shock tactics make sense – this is about saving lives, right? Well, yeah, maybe – that and snobbery. But where does this demonisation end?

Tip junk food into a trough and you're effectively saying the people who eat it are pigs: greedy ignorant livestock, who perhaps deserve pity, or perhaps scorn, but clearly don't deserve freedom of choice. Because left to their own devices, look what they'll do: they'll happily drink a five-litre bottle of cooking oil, like the woeful, **indolent** scum we think they are.

Glossary

Indolent Lazy.

1 Discuss with a partner the main arguments Brooker is presenting in Source 11. Use the following questions to support your discussion:
- Who or what does Charlie Brooker start by criticising?
- Who or what does he move on to criticise as his argument develops?
- What is his overall point ?
- Is there a counter-argument to his point of view?

You may find it useful to construct an argument tree to help you trace the argument (see page 116).

2 Look again at the list of language features on page 123. How many can you see in Source 11?

What have you learnt?

Comparison is one of the key skills for GCSE Reading non-fiction.

This is a typical GCSE-style comparative question:

Compare the ways in which the writers use language to present their point of view in Source 10 and Source 11. Give some examples and explain what the effects are.

Using your knowledge of how to structure a comparison and the type of comparative language to use (see page 119), plan and write a 200 word answer to this question. You should allow yourself 20 minutes to complete the task.

British Heart Foundation

What goes into crisps goes into you.

Some crisps contain 33% cooking oil. bhf.org.uk

Bridge to GCSE

Develop 'active reading' strategies now, in preparation for GCSE. Learn to read **critically**, considering the writer's viewpoint, the language and the presentational features of the text. Think about why they are used and what their effects are.

Check your level

LEVEL 6 I can easily identify relevant points and use well-chosen, appropriate quotation.

LEVEL 7 I can precisely identify relevant points and make close analytical reference to the text.

LEVEL 8 I can interpret and analyse texts critically, offering detailed, well-supported insights.

Learning objective

- To practise writing about a non-fiction text.

Bridge to GCSE

- At GCSE, you will be asked to write about two or three non-fiction texts in an exam or a controlled assessment.

In an exam or a controlled assessment you will usually be told what the 'source' of a text is (the form) and who wrote it. You may also be told where the source comes from: for example, a magazine, newspaper or website. However, identifying the audience and purpose will often be up to you, as will describing the way the writers have used language and presentational features to achieve their purpose.

Your task

Read Source 12, a newspaper report by Sophie Borland, from *The Daily Telegraph* newspaper.

Source 12

Glossy magazines face airbrush ban

Magazines could be banned from using airbrushed photographs of celebrities that make them look slimmer over fears that they are promoting unrealistic body images.

Editors from glossy publications including *Vogue*, *Hello!* and *Elle* are to meet to discuss best practice on using digitally enhanced pictures.

The Periodical Publishers Association (PPA), which represents the magazine industry, has said a series of discussions will be held.

The move follows criticisms by the Model Health Inquiry, which accused editors of acting irresponsibly and promoting a size-zero culture.

The report, released last September, urged the fashion industry to adopt a voluntary code on the use of computer technology to give models unrealistically perfect figures. […]

The use of digitally enhanced images of actresses such as Kate Winslet and Keira Knightley in magazines or to promote films has been criticised for its effect on women's body image. […]

Knightley's bust was noticeably enhanced on the US posters for the film *King Arthur* in 2004.

'Before' and 'after' images of Keira Knightley airbrushed for the film King Arthur.

The PPA announcement came on the same day as an expert in eating disorders claimed that society's obsession with being slim was encouraging diet-binge cycles and bulimia.

Prof Janet Treasure, of the Institute of Psychiatry at King's College London, said yesterday that people's brains could be permanently altered in the process, making them more susceptible to other addictions.

Now read Source 5 again, the article by Lucy Mangan on page 114.

You are going to compare the ways the writers of these two texts present their ideas.

Plan your response

You could compare
- the purpose of each text
- the audience each text is aimed at
- the form of each text
- the use of language features (choice of words, emotive language, statistics, sentence length and type, rhetorical techniques)
- the use of presentational features (headlines, images, captions, paragraph type and length)
- the structure and organisation of the texts
- the tone of each text – formal or informal, serious or humorous, shocking or comforting, emotive or neutral.

1 Using the list above, make a list of the similarities and differences between Source 12 and Source 5.

2 Try to add a short piece of evidence to each item on your list.

> **Bridge to GCSE**
>
> You should *always* use supporting evidence (quotations), even if the question doesn't mention it explicitly.

Write your response

Now it's time to complete your writing task.

Compare the ways in which the writers use language, structure and presentation to present their point of view in Source 12 and Source 5. Give some examples and explain what the effects are.

Checklist for success

✓ Make every word count.

✓ Support ideas with evidence.

✓ Comment, don't describe.

✓ Work quickly and purposefully.

> **Bridge to GCSE**
>
> To aim for a grade C and above at GCSE, you always need to comment on **how** and **why** features are used, not just describe what they are.

Learning objective

- To evaluate your strengths.
- To identify areas for development.

Bridge to GCSE

- Improve your work by reviewing the work of another student.

In this chapter you have been learning to

- **retrieve information and ideas**
- **understand and interpret meaning**
- **comment on the effectiveness of language**
- **comment on the effectiveness of presentational features in the texts**
- **select references and quotations from texts.**

You have learnt that non-fiction texts have a form, an audience and a purpose (or sometimes more than one purpose). You have also learnt that you need to look carefully at how language and presentational features have been used to achieve the purpose.

Top tip

Comparison questions want you to consider similarities and differences between two texts.

A strong Level 6 response would demonstrate the following:

- a clear understanding of the text with appropriate, relevant quotation
- detailed consideration of the effectiveness of particular language features
- detailed consideration of the effectiveness of particular presentational features
- clear engagement with ideas, interpreting ideas and starting to explore.

Here is how one student started their writing task.

> Source 12 is a newspaper article reporting on changes to how advertisers are allowed to use airbrushing. The article appears to be balanced because it gives lots of facts such as 'editors are to meet'. This makes the article sound like a report, giving a factual account. The text is written in the passive voice, using an impersonal tone: there is no personal engagement and we do not get any sense of the 'writer' of the text, her personality, or her opinion on the facts presented. Also, the style of language is very balanced.

Understands the text

Uses supporting evidence

Comments on the effect of language features

The second text is an article which is immediately much more one-sided. This article focuses on a similar issue; however the tone and style is much more personal and lively, giving the writer's opinions strongly with phrases like: 'it seems almost unfair' and 'standard of impossible perfection'. The language is much more emotive, as this writer is arguing a particular point of view rather than presenting an unbiased account of events.

Finds a similarity

Finds a difference

Develops the point with another difference

Comments on the effect of language features

s this piece of work a Level 6?

What could be improved in this piece of work? Set the student three targets.

Take one of the targets you have suggested. Write two or three sentences that the student could add to this piece of work. Your sentences might come at the end or in the middle of the paragraph.

Checklist for success

✓ Use your reading time well – keep a pencil in your hand, underline anything useful.

✓ If you have a good idea mid-sentence, jot it in the margin so you don't forget it.

✓ Make every word count – never describe and don't waffle.

✓ Find short, relevant appropriate evidence to support your points.

✓ Focus on the question.

✓ Comment, don't describe.

✓ Make a short plan and skills checklist for your task.

✓ Remember: comparison questions want you to find similarities as well as differences.

Top tip

Comparative connectives help organise comparison answers. *also, furthermore, however, nevertheless.*

Bridge to GCSE

Handwriting is not assessed at GCSE, but you need to write legibly and at speed. Practising getting your ideas down quickly is a very important part of exam preparation. Cursive script (joined-up handwriting) can help you to write quickly.

Check your progress

In this chapter you have learnt that identifying form, purpose and audience is the most important first step for reading non-fiction. You have developed the skill of following a writer's argument, considering how language, organisation and presentational features help a writer to communicate their ideas to a reader.

Taking it further

Read the points under each Level heading below. Which Level do you think you have reached in this chapter, and what do you need to do to improve?

LEVEL 5 (Aiming for GCSE C/B)

AF2 I can identify relevant parts of a text to comment on.

AF4 I can identify and explain how structure and form have been used.

AF5 I can identify the main purpose and viewpoint of a text.

LEVEL 6 (Aiming for GCSE B/A)

AF2 I can identify relevant parts of a text and use apt quotations to support my ideas.

AF4 I can comment on how a range of organisational and structural features have been used.

AF5 I can identify and explain the main purpose and viewpoint in a text and trace the way it develops.

LEVEL 7 (Aiming for GCSE A/A*)

AF2 I can select and use precise quotations to support my analysis of a text.

AF4 I can start to evaluate the way a text has been structured and organised to support its purpose.

AF5 I can analyse and evaluate the ways a writer has presented a viewpoint with detailed reference to the text.

Next steps to GCSE

At GCSE, you will be assessed on reading non-fiction in an examination or a controlled assessment. You will need to develop your ability to compare texts with each other, as this is one of the real differences between Key Stage 3 and GCSE.

Chapter 6

Writing non-fiction texts

In this chapter you will learn how to produce pieces of writing with a clear form, for a clear audience and purpose. You will develop the ways you structure and sequence your writing, and consider how to adapt the style and tone of your work to make it appropriate to the form, audience and purpose. In particular, you will focus on writing to argue and persuade.

Bridge to GCSE

To get you ready for your GCSE course, this chapter will take you through the following steps:

Explore ideas
- Adapt your writing to suit the form, audience and purpose.

Check your skills
- Structure and sequence your writing.

Extend your skills
- Make subtle use of persuasive techniques.

Plan and write
- Make and use effective plans, and practise writing under timed conditions.

Improve your work
- Review your response and set yourself a target for improvement.

Your GCSE-style assessment task will be a writing task to argue or persuade.

Key Stage 3 Writing Assessment Focuses		GCSE English/English Language Assessment Objectives	
AF2	Produce texts which are appropriate to task, reader and purpose	AO3/4i	Write to communicate clearly, effectively and imaginatively, using and adapting forms and selecting vocabulary appropriate to task and purpose in ways that engage the reader
AF3	Organise and present whole texts effectively, sequencing and structuring information, ideas and events	AO3/4ii	Organise information and ideas into structured and sequenced sentences, paragraphs and whole texts, using a variety of linguistic and structural features to support cohesion and overall coherence
AF4	Construct paragraphs and use cohesion within and between paragraphs		
AF5	Vary sentences for clarity, purpose and effect	AO3/4iii	Use a range of sentence structures for clarity, purpose and effect, with accurate punctuation and spelling

Learning objective

- To adapt your writing to the required form, audience and purpose.

Bridge to GCSE

- Part of your GCSE English examination will be to write in a specific form for a specific purpose.

Non-fiction writing is all around us – it is very likely that you read several non-fiction texts every day without even realising it. Learning to produce a forceful, memorable non-fiction text is an important skill for GCSE. Whether you are writing to inform, explain, argue or persuade, there are skills you can learn to make your writing precise, accurate and compelling.

Getting you thinking

Think about all the different types of non-fiction text you encountered in Chapter 5.

As a writer of non-fiction, you will always need to think about your **form** (what type of text it is), your **audience** (who it is for) and your **purpose** (what it is for).

- Read the following three items, which are first paragraphs of three different texts. Can you identify the form, the audience and the purpose of each item?

Bridge to GCSE

You may not be offered a choice of tasks in your exam, so you need to develop the ability to write in a range of different forms, for different audiences and purposes.

Source 1

> Good morning Year 9, it's a pleasure to be here today and see so many bright, interested faces in front of me. Now, as you know, this is the first day of your Healthy School Week, and I have been invited today to talk to you about body image. Now, who thinks they know what this means?

Source 2

> Dear Parent/Carer,
>
> Next week your son's/daughter's year group will be participating in Healthy School Week. The aim of the week is to engage in a range of curriculum activities designed to increase student awareness of the factors that can contribute to their physical, mental and emotional health. Students will be following a structured timetable of activities, some of which will be delivered by subject specialists within school. We are also lucky enough to have some very exciting visiting speakers who will be delivering workshops on nutrition, self-esteem and body image.

Source 3

The vast majority of the media these days seems to be convinced that all of us are overweight, slobbing-about sacks of lard who need a constant stream of stern tellings-off, gut-churning shock tactics and a constant bombardment of images of stick-thin, bordering on anorexic 'celebrities' showing us how we just, don't quite, and aren't likely to ever (sorry) measure up to the ideal. And is it working? Are we becoming a micro-version of the sports-obsessed New Zealanders? Are we sylph-like, athletic gods and goddesses? Or do the latest NHS statistics released this week demonstrate that the country is sliding ever-faster towards an obesity crisis of quite enormous (no pun intended) proportions. Or portions.

GCSE skills focus

A successful piece of writing is one which uses an appropriate tone and register. The tone you create will be influenced by the level of formality in your writing.

Every time you write a non-fiction text, it is important to think about how formal or informal your language should be. You need to judge for yourself which tone to use – it depends on who the audience is, the writer's relationship with the audience and the purpose of the writing.

- An informal tone is often used for a younger audience, or for friends and peers. Informal writing is often lighthearted, 'chatty' and friendly, can use humour and possibly more **colloquial language**.

- A formal tone is more often used for people you don't know, a serious subject, or for impersonal matters such as business transactions, complaints or information. It will use **standard English** forms.

 Key terms

Colloquial language Words and phrases belonging to everyday conversational language, including contractions and slang.

Standard English Accepted, agreed forms of grammar, vocabulary and spelling, as found in text books and official documents.

Non-standard English Grammar, words and spelling that vary from the accepted 'correct' form, including local dialects and regional variations.

Now you try it

1 Rank the following text types according to how **formal** or **informal** you think the language should be:

- speech to a Year 9 assembly

- letter to parents/carers about Healthy School Week

- broadsheet newspaper article about obesity

- leaflet for Year 3 students about healthy eating

- magazine article for teenagers about attitudes to body size

- advice sheet for parents on body image.

Write down at least one reason for each decision.

2 Look at the following list of features:

- direct address to an audience

- first person

- rhetorical techniques

- lists of information

- use of humour

- friendly tone

- reference to recent events

- complex, formal language and sentence structure.

Decide which of the features would appear in the following texts:

- a leaflet for Year 3 students about why eating '5 a day' is important

- a magazine article aimed at teenagers with the title: 'Healthy or Skinny: Which is Best?'

- an advice sheet for parents on how to improve their teenage son's/daughter's body image.

Taking it further

Working in pairs or small groups, discuss the three texts listed at the bottom of the previous page. How would you make each text suitable for its audience and purpose? Think about

- tone
- vocabulary
- layout and presentational features
- organisational features
- structure
- techniques you might use.

Choose one of the three texts that you have discussed. Write the first paragraph or short section of this text.

To write good non-fiction texts, bear in mind the points below.

Top tip

Use a range and variety of sentences to make your writing sound polished and confident. Short sentences can be used to emphasise points, while complex sentences can provide information and detail. (See page 14 of Chapter 1 for a reminder of the three main sentence types.)

Checklist for success

✓ Organise your material to suit the form, audience and purpose.

✓ Adapt your vocabulary to suit your audience and purpose.

✓ Adapt your sentence structure to suit your audience and purpose.

✓ Think about how to make the tone of your writing appeal to your audience.

What have you learnt?

Share your work with a partner. Read his or her work and see if you can decide which text type your partner has chosen. Pick three things about the writing that made the text type clear.

Bridge to GCSE

When you are asked to write a non-fiction text, especially in an exam, you may be asked to inform/explain, or argue/persuade.

Check your level

LEVEL 5 I can use an appropriate style and tone to match the purpose.

LEVEL 6 I can write with an appropriate level of formality with some effective use of devices.

LEVEL 7 I can consistently control the level of formality of my writing by using a range of devices.

Using the correct register

Learning objective

- To consider how to adapt the register of your writing.

Bridge to GCSE

- At GCSE you are assessed on your ability to adapt your writing to suit the form, audience and purpose (FAP).

'Register' means your tone and level of formality. You may have some fantastic ideas and powerful content to present, but you also need to 'package' your ideas in the appropriate form. Using the right register demonstrates that you understand the audience and purpose of your work and can adapt your writing accordingly.

Getting you thinking

1 Which one of these non-fiction texts would use a formal register and which would use an informal register?

Text Type	Formal register	Informal register
An email to your best friend about your holiday		
A letter of complaint to a mobile phone company		
An article in your school magazine from the Student Council, welcoming new Year 7 students to your school		
An advice leaflet for the elderly on how to keep warm during cold weather		
An article in a scientific journal about recent studies of the earth's core temperature		

There are lots of ways to adapt your register. You might

- choose colloquial or standard English
- alter the level of difficulty of your vocabulary
- alter the length and complexity of the sentences you use
- change the narrative voice (first, second or third person).

See if you can think of any other things to add to this list. In what other ways might you adapt your writing if you want to use a specific register?

Bridge to GCSE

Considering the audience for your text is very important. If you can demonstrate that you have adapted your level of formality (or register) to suit that particular audience, you are starting to write like a GCSE student.

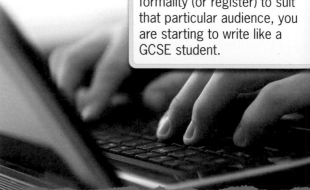

GCSE skills focus

Formal writing is usually serious and purposeful. It is often written in an **impersonal style**. It follows the rules of standard English. Sometimes the vocabulary and sentence structures are quite sophisticated, particularly if the text is aimed at educated adults. It is usual to assume the writer doesn't know the reader, and that the target audience is a group of people rather than one particular person. Sometimes a formal tone is appropriate even when the audience is someone you know. It depends on the nature of the text and the relationship between the writer and reader.

How to write impersonally:

- Minimise the use of first person – 'I think/believe/feel'.
- Use formal verbs – 'consider' rather than 'think about'.
- Try to replace less formal, emotive verbs with more formal ones – 'I am concerned' is more impersonal than 'I'm really worried about'.
- Avoid emotional expressions and emotive language.
- Be objective – 'it has been argued that' or 'it could be suggested that'.

 Key terms

Impersonal style Used when the writer doesn't know the person they are writing to, or when it is appropriate to keep a distance between reader and writer.

Informal writing is often more friendly and personal. It may not always follow all the rules of standard English and may use some non-standard English deliberately, for effect. It may be written in the first person, and sometimes it may have one particular person or group of people as its intended audience.

Sometimes the intended audience is someone known to the writer, such as a friend. Other texts might intentionally try to create a personal connection with the reader, as in some persuasive texts – for example, charity direct mail letters.

Deliberate use of non-standard English can be powerful if it is consciously used to appeal to a specific audience, such as a close friend or a group of teenagers. It can also be used ironically, for effect.

Now you try it

Read the following non-fiction text, which is an extract from a national newspaper report.

Results of a recent survey commissioned by the Health Ministry and published this week have uncovered some alarming statistics: over 75% of children between the ages of eight and fifteen not only consume less than 30% of the governmental recommendation of vitamin-rich foods per week, but 43% of this group actually consume less than 5%.

These foods, including fruits, vegetables, whole-grains, whole dairy products and fresh fish and poultry, are 'rarely seen on the plates of over 40% of the young people in this country', states the summative findings of the report's author, Dr Mary Benedict.

The Health Minister is due to be investigating ways to improve the Ministry's communication regarding the benefits to the nation's health of a balanced diet. The Education Secretary is expected to release details next week of its plans for 'Curriculum 2012', which proposes a radical overhaul of the ways in which health and nutrition are taught in schools.

Notice the use of 'expert' opinions and statistics to add strength to the argument.

1 Rewrite the report as it might appear in a magazine aimed at teenagers. See how you can adapt the following:

- use of voice (first person, second person, third person)
- use of tense (past tense, present tense)
- vocabulary
- tone (impersonal, personal)
- sentence structure.

Bridge to GCSE

Writing in a consistent narrative voice (for example, first person or third person) is a key feature of Level 5 writing. It also helps you to achieve Grade C at GCSE.

What have you learnt?

1 Share your work with a partner. Compare notes on how you adapted the text to suit a different audience.

2 What did you notice? What did your partner do particularly successfully? What do they need to do to improve?

Check your level

LEVEL 5 I can adapt my form to suit the purpose and maintain reader interest throughout.

LEVEL 6 I can create an appropriate tone and use devices most of the time to suit the level of formality.

LEVEL 7 I can successfully control and maintain the level of formality.

Learning objective

- To investigate ways of organising and developing ideas in a piece of writing to argue and persuade.

Bridge to GCSE

- The way you structure ideas can have a powerful effect on the reader. Use of structure is assessed at GCSE.

Writing to argue or persuade can be really powerful, as well as great fun to produce. Persuasive writing aims to 'win over' the audience, while argumentative writing states a case and has much more of a 'take it or leave it' attitude. Learning how to argue and persuade will be useful for lots of different situations, not just for passing GCSE exams.

Getting you thinking

What is an **argument**?

The famous *Monty Python* 'Argument' sketch has its own definition.

> M: Oh look, this isn't an argument.
> A: Yes it is.
> M: No it isn't. It's just contradiction.
> A: No it isn't.
> M: It is!
> A: It is not.
> M: Look, you just contradicted me.
> A: I did not.
> M: Oh you did!!
> A: No, no, no.
> M: You did just then.
> A: Nonsense!
> M: Oh, this is futile!
> A: No it isn't.
> M: I came here for a good argument.
> A: No you didn't; no, you came here for an argument.
> M: An argument isn't just contradiction.
> A: It can be.
> M: No it can't. An argument is a connected series of statements intended to establish a proposition.
> A: No it isn't.

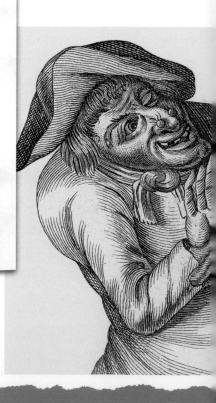

Working in groups, discuss the following:

- In the *Monty Python* sketch, who do you agree with, A or M, and why? Or are they both right (or wrong)?
- Come up with your own definition of what an 'argument' is, and describe some of its essential features.

GCSE skills focus

There are similarities between writing to persuade and writing to argue, and some of the same techniques can be used for both purposes.

Persuasive texts try to get their audience to change in some way: either their beliefs, their attitudes, or their actions. In a persuasive text you would expect to see a range of rhetorical techniques employed in order to work on the audience in subtle ways to alter their course of action. Persuasive texts can be more one-sided and emotive than argument texts.

According to *Monty Python*, an argument is 'a connected series of statements intended to establish a proposition'. **Argument texts** should present a well-considered point of view or line of reasoning, and provide evidence to demonstrate the strength and validity of the argument. Balance and tact are important terms to consider – you need to consider the counter-argument before tactfully and logically refuting it.

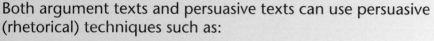

> **Top tip**
>
> Drawing on expert opinions and statistical evidence can reinforce the strength of your argument.

Both argument texts and persuasive texts can use persuasive (rhetorical) techniques such as:

- rhetorical questions (to draw the reader in)
- hyperbole (exaggeration)
- list of three (three adjectives or phrases in a series, to intensify the point)
- imagery (similes, metaphors)

- repetition
- offering a counter-argument in order to refute it
- considering an alternative point of view.

A typical **argument text** might, for example, be a newspaper article arguing for a review of the government's health policy, or an article in a music magazine about the rise in illegal downloading.

A typical **persuasive text** might be a speech made during a party political broadcast prior to an election, or any form of advertising.

> **Bridge to GCSE**
>
> At GCSE it is likely that you will be asked to produce writing to either argue or persuade – and sometimes both. This is because the two forms of writing can be doing similar jobs.

Now you try it

You are going to use an argument tree to structure and organise ideas for the following task.

Some people believe that unhealthy foods such as white bread, chips and chocolate should be taxed by the government in the same way as cigarettes and alcohol. Write an article for a school magazine arguing for or against this idea.

- £5 million are spent by the NHS every year treating obesity-related illnesses.

- People get into bad habits and the tax will help them break these.

The main trunk of the argument and three branches (paragraphs) have been filled in for you. You also have some 'twigs' filled in. The twigs are the development points of each branch.

1 The following six development points need to be added to the argument tree. Copy the tree and add the following six points to the correct branches.

- Unhealthy foods will become less 'normal' and acceptable.
- When people start to see the benefits of the tax they will be grateful it was imposed in the first place.
- Healthy foods may become cheaper and more easily available.
- The tax will encourage parents to be firmer about what their children eat.
- The money saved could also be used to cut taxes in other places for poorer people.
- Organic foods are expensive, as they are only grown by small producers.

2 Consider offering a counter-argument or alternative point of view to each branch, in order to show that you have considered alternative arguments.

Taking it further

Use your argument tree to make a paragraph plan for a piece of writing:

- Paragraph 1 – your main **thesis** (argument), your point of view
- Paragraph 2 – branch 1 arguments (and counter-argument)
- Paragraph 3 – branch 2 arguments (and counter-argument)
- Paragraph 4 – branch 3 arguments (and counter-argument)
- Paragraph 5 – conclusion, returns to the main point and summarises how you have proved your thesis.

Key terms

Thesis Overall idea, or argument, developed in a piece of non-fiction writing.

The statements on each branch become the topic sentences for each paragraph. These show the reader how your argument is developing.

Connectives are vital to developing a structured, sequenced line of argument.

Types of connectives	Examples
Connectives that develop an argument	also, additionally, furthermore, moreover
Connectives that introduce a different point of view	however, whereas, on the other hand, conversely, nevertheless, in spite of this
'Cause and effect' connectives	if… then…, consequently, ultimately, in the end, therefore, as a result

Top tip

When you are writing, vary the range of sentences you use for deliberate effect. Introduce some sophisticated punctuation such as semi-colons, which can be used to balance sentences. They are extremely useful in 'cause and effect' sentences.

What have you learnt?

Swap your paragraph plan with a partner. How effective is their paragraph plan? Could you use it yourself to write a response to this task? Give the plan a mark out of 10 based on how useful and detailed you think it is.

Check your level

LEVEL 5 I can organise my ideas into clear paragraphs with some links between them.

LEVEL 6 I can use paragraphs and topic sentences to signal the overall direction of the text.

LEVEL 7 I can skilfully use a range of paragraphs and other features for effect.

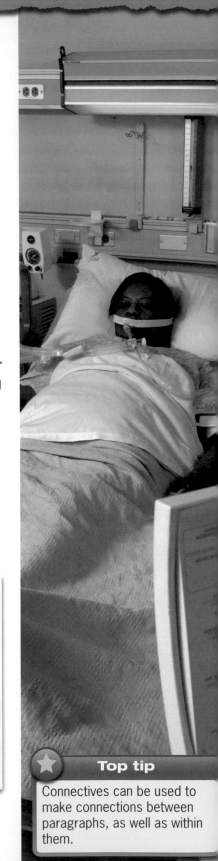

Learning objective

- To learn how to structure an effective, developed paragraph in an argument text.

Bridge to GCSE

- At GCSE, your paragraph structure and organisation will be assessed, particularly in your English Literature and Language exam papers.

One way of assessing good organisation is to read the introduction, the conclusion and the topic sentence of each paragraph. You know that it is important to have a clear structure to your whole text – your introduction, your main points and your conclusion. Structuring and organising each individual paragraph is also very important.

Getting you thinking

Paragraphs are used to organise and separate your ideas. Using them accurately and deliberately demonstrates your ability to think logically and clearly.

A whole paragraph should contain a complete, developed thought. **Topic sentences** introduce the idea of the paragraph. The rest of the paragraph develops that idea, giving examples and reinforcing the main idea.

1 Look at this example of a paragraph and see if you can identify the topic sentence and the three development points.

> Obesity is costing the country a fortune. Every year the NHS releases statistics that compare how much of their funding is spent on treating illnesses related to obesity, such as diabetes and heart disease. If people had more healthy diets in the first place, then this would reduce the amount of diet-related illnesses and therefore put less strain on NHS resources. Furthermore, the money saved treating obesity could be used to treat other life-threatening illnesses such as cancer.

2 Can you spot three examples of connectives used to develop ideas? Look back at the list of connectives in the last lesson (page 143) to help you.

Top tip

Connectives can be used to make connections between paragraphs, as well as within them.

GCSE skills focus

Topic sentences are like subheadings: they summarise the point of the paragraph.

The rest of the paragraph illustrates the main point, by using

- an example, such as an anecdote from real life
- a quotation or testimonial from a respected person such as a doctor or scientist
- facts, quotations from experts or witnesses, and statistics.

Bridge to GCSE

Using facts, quotes and statistics is very powerful. For a writing task you are allowed to invent them – you are not expected to be an expert on every topic you are asked to write about.

Now you try it

You are going to write your own paragraph using a topic sentence and reinforcement. You have a choice of three topic sentences to work from:

a The media has an enormous influence on the way young people feel about themselves.

b If the government want people to be more healthy, they should cut the cost of healthy foods.

c The education system could do more to educate young people about health and nutrition.

- You should aim to add **three** sentences to your topic sentence.
- You should aim to use at least two connectives to help develop your points.

Top tip

Exclamation marks tend to be overused. Avoid them unless you are convinced it will strengthen your work.

What have you learnt?

Swap your paragraph with a partner. Highlight the topic sentence first of all. Then give one mark for each development point and each connective used. See which of you has gained the most points from this activity.

Set your partner a target for improvement using the Level checker below.

Top tip

Newspaper reports often use what are known as tabloid paragraphs. A tabloid paragraph is a single-sentence paragraph, which breaks down the information into easy chunks.

Check your level

LEVEL 5	I can write a clearly structured paragraph.
LEVEL 6	I can control and sequence my ideas within my paragraphs.
LEVEL 7	I can craft well-constructed and interesting paragraphs.

Learning objective

- To learn to use rhetorical techniques in a sophisticated way.

Bridge to GCSE

- At GCSE, adapting your writing to suit a particular FAP includes using the conventions of a particular text type with skill and subtlety.

The expression 'language is power' has a lot to do with *rhetoric*, which has been used since the time of the ancient Greeks. Modern-day journalists, public speakers and politicians all use the techniques of rhetoric in their written and spoken communication.

Getting you thinking

Powerful persuasive texts share a number of key attributes:

- the writer is trying to get the audience to change in some way; either their beliefs, their attitudes, or their actions
- they are often more one-sided and emotive than argumentative
- the rhetorical techniques are often very subtle and designed to work on an emotional level.

Here is an example of rhetoric from a famous orator (public speaker), the US President, Barack Obama.

For we have a choice in this country. We can accept a politics that breeds division, and conflict, and cynicism. […]

We can do that.

But if we do, I can tell you that in the next election, we'll be talking about some other distraction. And then another one. And then another one. And nothing will change.

That is one option. Or, at this moment, in this election, we can come together and say, 'Not this time.' This time we want to talk about the crumbling schools that are stealing the future of black children and white children and Asian children and Hispanic children and Native American children. This time we want to reject the cynicism that tells us that these kids can't learn; that those kids who don't look like us are somebody else's problem. The children of America are not those kids, they are our kids, and we will not let them fall behind in a 21st century economy. Not this time.

In this speech Obama uses rhetorical techniques with real skill and subtlety.

- Read the notes on the next page. Then make a list of the techniques you can find in Obama's speech and provide a short quotation to support each one.

GCSE skills focus

The term 'rhetoric' means 'the art of persuasion' or 'the art of public speaking'. It is known as an 'art', as there are specific techniques, which can be learned. These include:

- rhetorical questions
- list of three
- **hyperbole**
- flattery
- **pathos**
- repetition
- emotive language
- imagery
- **anecdote**
- **alliteration**
- inclusive pronouns ('we' rather than 'you' or 'I')
- powerful, well-crafted sentences, using punctuation for effect.

Key terms

Hyperbole Exaggeration for emphasis or effect.

Pathos Language aimed at arousing sympathy or pity.

Anecdote An amusing or interesting story, often personal.

Alliteration Use of words with the same starting sound placed near each other.

Now you try it

Use the list of techniques you have identified to write a short speech of your own, on any topic that is particularly important for you, either serious or light-hearted.

Aim to use as many rhetorical techniques as you can, but, like Obama, be subtle. Overusing rhetorical techniques can make your writing sound clumsy and awkward.

What have you learnt?

Test your speech by reading it to an audience, either a partner or your class. See how many rhetorical techniques they spot. Ask for some feedback on whether you managed to 'win them over'.

Check your level

LEVEL 6	I can use a range of devices to suit my purpose.
LEVEL 7	I can control a range of devices successfully and subtly to suit my purpose.
LEVEL 8	I can select and adapt devices with distinctive personal style.

Learning objective

● To produce an effective plan for a persuasive piece of writing.

Bridge to GCSE

● At GCSE you will use structure and organise your ideas to support the point you are making.

An effective non-fiction text should be well structured and sequenced. You need to decide your direction and have your conclusion clearly thought out before you start.

Your task

The box below contains your writing task for this chapter.

> *As many of the problems and issues young people face are caused by low levels of self-esteem, schools should adapt what they teach to provide lessons on body image and confidence for teenagers.*
>
> *Write an article for a magazine arguing either **for** or **against** this idea.*

You will have 45 minutes and should aim to write about two sheets of A4 paper or 400 words.

GCSE skills focus

Look at the following list of skills:

● Write a clear response to the task set.
● Write in an appropriate way for purpose and audience throughout.
● Organise your writing into paragraphs and sentences.
● Use punctuation, grammar and spelling correctly.
● Employ standard English appropriately.

When you are writing non-fiction texts, these are the things the person marking your work is looking for. Working with a partner, choose the most important key words in the list above and make a note of them.

In an exam or controlled assessment situation you need to work quickly and effectively.

The first thing to do is to underline or highlight key words in the question and identify the FAP. Have a look at how one student has done this on the next page. Working with a partner, discuss whether you could use any of these notes for your own article.

Plan and write

Needs expanding – talk about causes? Media pressure, celebrity culture, focus on material possessions?

Argue for this – need ideas – what about lessons on nutrition, confidence-building, more PE?

Argue for idea but also suggest that it's only one way of supporting teenagers and that there may be others

As many of the problems and issues young people face are caused by low levels of self-esteem, schools should adapt what they teach to provide lessons on body image and confidence for teenagers.

Write an article for a teenage magazine arguing either *for* or *against* this idea.

Think of some problems – drugs, drinking, not working hard at school, eating issues, being unfit...

Talk about other ways society could help?

Audience is teenagers so use 'us' and 'we' and make it not too formal

Here is another student's plan. How could it be improved?

Why they have low self-esteem

Things teenagers suffer from

Article: young people's self-esteem problems in schools

What schools can do to help

Remember FAP

Paragraphs

Interesting vocabulary

Plan and write your response

Construct an argument tree for your own task:

- Top of the tree = ideas for your introduction
- Main trunk = the question
- Three branches = topic sentences you are going to use
- Two or three twigs on each branch = ways you are going to develop each topic sentence
- Bottom of the tree = ideas for your conclusion

Remember to mention alternative points of view to show that you are presenting a considered argument.

Now it's time to complete your writing task.

Checklist for success

✓ Concentrate on your structure and organisation.
✓ Keep your point of view clear.
✓ Make each point into a developed paragraph.
✓ Work quickly and purposefully.

Reading and reflecting

Learning objective

- To evaluate your strengths.
- To identify areas for development.

Bridge to GCSE

- At GCSE you will learn what to look for when you are reading over your own work.

Now that you have completed your writing task you should be much more confident about how to present a point of view clearly and consistently, structuring and organising your ideas and deliberately using techniques to argue your case.

Getting you thinking

Look at the following example of student work:

> It would be good if schools taught students some ways of developing self-esteem. Some of the subjects taught in schools aren't that relevant any more. The whole curriculum needs bringing up to date. Schools are the ones who suffer if the results aren't good. Results would go up if the teenagers felt better about themselves. It would also improve attendance. You are more likely to want to come to school if it is a place that makes you feel good about yourself.

1 Discuss with a partner:
   - Is the text accurately punctuated?
   - Does it link to the task clearly?
   - Does it have a clear topic sentence?
   - Do the rest of the sentences develop the topic sentence?
   - Do the sentence structures make it boring to read?

   You should have answered 'yes' to all of these questions.

2 Working either on your own or with your partner, rewrite this paragraph to make a more persuasive text. Use the checklist below to help you.

Bridge to GCSE

Interesting and accurate sentence structures, accurate punctuation and spelling are usually worth around one third of the marks in a writing task.

Top tip

Using a mixture of short and long (simple and complex) sentences deliberately for effect will improve your writing style.

Checklist for success

✓ Use more complex sentences, adding some subordinate clauses.
✓ Use at least one rhetorical question.
✓ Use some short sentences for effect.
✓ Use some connectives, colons and semi colons.

Have a look at this piece of writing. All the punctuation has been removed.

> whenever you pick up a magazine turn on the tv or go online these days you are bombarded with images of tiny little stick people wearing designer clothes carrying designer bags and sporting designer shades this makes us normal people feel fat poor and pathetic this can have a devastating effect on the average persons self esteem its time to change the media need to take more responsibility for the message they are sending out every day at the other end of the scale you get the magazines pointing accusing figures at celebrities who have a bit of a tummy or cellulite or have put a few pounds on what do they want is it any wonder we are all suffering with low self esteem

3 Rewrite this paragraph, inserting capital letters, full stops, commas, question marks, hyphens and apostrophes so that it makes sense.

Bridge to GCSE

You do not have to be a perfect speller to get high marks at GCSE, but clear and interesting punctuation can make all the difference. Top candidates use the full range of punctuation for deliberate effect.

What have you learnt?

Read the paragraph you have written.
What Level would you give the paragraph?

Check your level	**LEVEL 5**	I can use a full range of punctuation accurately, including commas to mark clauses.
	LEVEL 6	I can use a full range of punctuation in a variety of different sentence structures.
	LEVEL 7	I can use a variety of sentence types and punctuation deliberately to create effects.

Check your progress

In this chapter you have considered how to adapt your writing to suit a given form, audience and purpose. You have learnt about altering your register to suit a variety of audiences. You have considered the differences between writing to argue and writing to persuade, and practised ways of planning a structured argument.

Taking it further

Read the points under each Level heading below. Which Level do you think you have reached in this chapter, and what do you need to do to improve?

LEVEL 5 (Aiming for GCSE C/B)

AF2   I can write clearly and appropriately for the purpose and form showing a clear awareness of the reader.

AF3   I can write using an appropriate structure and sequence material clearly.

AF4   I can use paragraphs to structure the main ideas in my writing.

AF5/6 I can vary my sentence lengths, punctuation and structure to make my ideas clear.

LEVEL 6 (Aiming for GCSE B/A)

AF2   I can consistently maintain the purpose and style of my writing to suit my audience.

AF3   I can control and sequence my material, using a clear structure.

AF4   I can construct paragraphs to clearly support my meaning and purpose.

AF5/6 I can use a full range of punctuation and sentence structures consistently and accurately.

LEVEL 7 (Aiming for GCSE A/A*)

AF2   I can successfully adapt my writing to suit the form and control the effects on the reader.

AF3   I can skilfully shape and manage the structure and sequence of my writing.

AF4   I can use paragraphing as an integral part of my meaning.

AF5/6 I can use a variety of sentence types and punctuation to shape and craft sentences.

Next steps to GCSE

For GCSE, you will be applying these skills in an examination or controlled assessment. You will have to plan quickly and effectively. You will get better marks if you adapt your writing to the FAP and make every word count.

Chapter 7

Studying spoken language

In this chapter you will explore a wide range of issues around spoken language. These include the differences between speech and writing, different attitudes to spoken language, how you speak and what other people think about it, and how people adapt their speech in different situations and spoken genres.

Bridge to GCSE

To get you ready for your GCSE course, this chapter will take you through the following steps:

Explore ideas

- Understand the difference between speech and writing.
- Recognise and describe significant details and features of spoken language, using correct technical vocabulary.

Check your skills

- Understand how context influences spoken language.

Extend your skills

- Analyse two transcripts as examples of a particular spoken genre.

Plan and write

- Write a detailed and focused analysis.

Improve your work

For your GCSE-style assessment task you will have two choices:

1 Analyse your idiolect (the way you speak and how you adapt it in different situations).

2 Explore the spoken genre of sports commentary.

Key Stage 3 Speaking and Listening Assessment Focuses	GCSE English Language Assessment Objectives
AF4 Understand the range and uses of spoken language, commenting on meaning and impact […]	AO2i Understand variations in spoken language, explaining why language changes in relation to contexts
	AO2ii Evaluate the impact of spoken language choices in their own and others' use

What is spoken language?

Learning objective

- To explore the differences between speech and writing.

Bridge to GCSE

- At GCSE you will be asked to research and write about one aspect of spoken language. You will need to understand some of the main differences between the way we speak and the way we write.

Every day you use several different forms of communication, mostly without thinking about it. You will already be familiar with analysing written texts. You might not be so familiar with analysing the way you and other people speak.

Getting you thinking

Look at the following texts. For each one decide:

- Is it written or spoken?
- How do you know?

Text 1

The full moon rose over the dark, craggy mountains bathing the castle and its surroundings in a sinister grey light. In the distance a lone wolf howled as if warning me to turn back. I had to continue, to enter the castle and to reveal the dark secrets that lay inside.

Text 2

anyway I saw you know Ian and he was er basically in a right state yeh that's right crying and everything so I went up I asked him what was wrong and er he said that she'd dumped him no warning or nothing she was seeing this other lad

Text 3

hi mum cn u get me im @ ians bout 8 ta xxx

154

GCSE skills focus

Speech and writing are different **modes** of communication. They have some things in common but each one has its own features.

Look at the Venn diagram below.

Writing

Speech

Is mainly **permanent**

Tends to be planned

Uses **grammar**, vocabulary and sentence structure to create meaning

Usually follows grammatical rules

The audience is usually absent

Stays focused on one topic

Changes according to purpose and audience

Can be formal or informal

Is mainly **transient**

Tends to be **spontaneous**

Uses many features of written language, but can be made more expressive with tone of voice and gestures

Does not always follow grammatical rules

The audience is usually present

Involves taking turns with other speakers

Did you notice that Text 3 was harder to define? Look at it again:

hi mum cn u get me im @ ians bout 8 ta xxx

It does not seem to fit with either the description of speech or of writing in the diagram. This is because it is a text message, which is a **multimodal** form. New forms of technology, such as mobile phones and the internet, have created new modes of communication. Multimodal forms contain some features of speech, some features of writing, and some features of their own.

- Look at the text message again. Can you find features of speech and features of writing in the text?

Now you try it

Now it's time to think about how you use language. Look at the table below, which was completed by a Year 9 student. In the 'Comment' column the student describes and explains how he adapts his language when using different modes.

1 Some boxes have been left empty or incomplete – make your own notes to complete the table.

Mode	Example	Comment
Writing 1	Writing a Gothic horror story in English	• Make my writing interesting by choosing the right type of exaggerated vocabulary • Hook the reader by adding clues and using page-turners • Plan my writing before I start so I know how the story will end • Be careful with spelling and punctuation because it will affect my grade
Writing 2	Leaving a note for my mum	• Don't write in sentences. Just get my meaning across as quickly as possible. • Use abbreviations • Leave kisses if I want something or have done something wrong
Speech 1	Asking for something in a shop	• Tend to be polite and quite formal - more likely to get what I want that way
Speech 2	Chatting to friends	
Multimodal 1	Text to Grandma	• Don't always use full sentences because texts have to be brief but still use punctuation • Use some abbreviations but not as many as I use with my friends because my nan has only just started using her mobile phone
Multimodal 2	Social networking	

2 Working in pairs, come up with new examples of the three main types of text:

- written - spoken - multimodal.

Create a new table like the one above, and add comments in the third column describing the key features of each text.

> **Bridge to GCSE**
>
> At GCSE, you will have to find source material to analyse for your spoken language study. Analysing your own use of language is a good starting point.

Taking it further

Generally, speech that is more formal will follow the rules of grammar more closely. Speech that is less formal will contain more **slang** and will not follow the rules of grammar so closely.

When you look at an example of spoken language, a good starting point is to decide how formal you think it is. This will influence lots of things like vocabulary, grammar and structure. The formality of language is often due to the situation or **context** in which it happens.

Key terms

Slang Informal words or figures of speech; may be popular for a short period of time; generally not regional. For example, 'wheels' and 'motor' are widely used slang terms for car.

Context The circumstances in which something takes place.

1 Look at the following situations and rank them according to how formal or informal you think they are:

- Asking for help in a shop
- Answering questions at a job interview
- Texting a friend
- Reporting on the TV news
- Instant messaging with friends
- Chatting with family members
- A teacher explaining a lesson to a class
- Giving a talk in assembly

What have you learnt?

Answer the following questions to check your understanding so far:

1 What are three of the main differences between speech and writing?

2 Can you find three examples of multimodal communication?

Check your level

LEVEL 5	I can explain the main differences between spoken and written language.
LEVEL 6	I can describe a range of differences between different modes of language.
LEVEL 7	I can analyse differences between different modes of language.

Learning objective

- To identify reasons why different people talk in different ways.
- To explore how and why the way you speak changes in different situations.
- To learn how to read a transcript.

Bridge to GCSE

- At GCSE you may choose to explore your own spoken language – what influences it and how it changes in different situations or contexts. You will also look at the way other people speak.

You have your own **idiolect** or individual way of speaking. Lots of things, such as where you come from, your family and your friends, influence your idiolect.

Getting you thinking

What influences the way you speak? How do you adapt the way you speak in different situations or contexts?

Complete a table like the one below:

| Where do you come from? |
| Do you have an **accent**? |
| Give examples of **dialect** words you use |
| Give examples of slang words you use |
| Do you speak differently with different members of your family? Give examples |
| Do you speak differently with your friends? Give examples |
| How do you speak in school? Give examples |
| Do you use any **jargon** to do with particular hobbies or interests, such as sport, computer games, music, dancing, skateboarding? |

 Key terms

Accent The way words are pronounced – often varies considerably and is highly regional.

Dialect The way vocabulary and word order changes in different parts of the world. For example, Geordie, Cockney, Australian.

Jargon Specialised language to do with a topic; for example, 'riff', 'bassline', 'garage' and 'soundcheck' are all examples of jargon to do with music.

GCSE skills focus

You must look carefully at the context of any piece of spoken language when you analyse it. In other words, what was the situation when the extract was spoken?

Within our own idiolect, we adapt the way we speak according to different situations. For example, you will probably speak differently – using a more formal **register**, closer to **Standard English** – with a teacher than with one of your friends.

 Key terms

Register Types of language used in different situations or contexts.

Standard English Accepted, agreed forms of grammar, vocabulary and pronunciation, as found in more formal situations such as reading the news or making a presentation.

When we choose a register, we usually consider four main things: **audience**, **purpose**, **topic** and **form**.

Audience	The person we are talking to affects our register. We might speak more respectfully and formally to someone in authority, like a police officer, and more informally when chatting with a friend or texting a brother or sister.
Purpose	Why we are talking affects our register and vocabulary. We will talk differently if we are giving instructions, commenting on a TV show or attempting to persuade someone to do something for us.
Topic	The topic or subject we are talking about will affect our choices of vocabulary and the meanings of words.
Form	It could be an interview, an informal conversation, an email, or a Tweet. Each form has its own rules, or conventions.

Extracts of spoken language are written down as **transcripts**. They are designed to reflect what was said as closely as possible rather than convert speech so that it follows the rules or written language.

- Punctuation and grammatical features, such as capital letters at the beginning of sentences, are not generally used.
- Pauses are important and are shown using brackets.
- Gestures can also be shown, using square brackets [ ]; they often convey important information about the speaker's attitude.

2 Different ways of speaking

Now you try it

This transcript is of a geography teacher introducing a lesson about rivers to a Year 9 class.

> ok guys (.) is everyone listening (.) there's too much chatting in that back corner [looks at back corner] (3) that's better (.) today's learning objective is to investigate the different stages of a river's journey to the sea (.) look at the sheet on your desk [holds sheet up] (1) it shows a river but there aren't any labels (.) what we're going to do is add labels (.) label 1 [points at label 1] shows where the river starts (.) can anyone tell me what this bit of the river's called (2) John what about you
>
> (.) micropause (less than a second)
>
> (2) two second pause
>
> [gesture]

1 Analyse this extract in groups. Make notes, commenting on
- audience
- purpose
- topic
- form
- level of formality
- specific language uses.

2 Using the extract above to guide you, write two short transcripts in which:

a you explain to your friend how you broke a window in your headteacher's office

b you explain to your headteacher how you broke a window in her (or his) office.

Remember to use an appropriate **register** for each transcript.

What have you learnt?

This is a 14 year-old boy describing his own idiolect.

> I come from Sheffield in South Yorkshire. I don't think I have a very strong accent but when I talk to people from other parts of the country, they tell me I do. I do use some dialect words. For example, I say 'right' (pronounced 'rate') instead of 'very' or 'really', for instance 'that was a right good goal'. My parents and grandparents use more dialect than me so my grandad says 'mashing tea' for 'making tea'. I still understand what he means but some of my friends wouldn't. I use different words with my friends. If someone is really muscular, we say they are 'hench' or 'ripped'. My grandparents wouldn't understand this but I think most fifteen-year-olds would no matter what part of the country they come from.
>
> I change the way I speak depending on who I'm talking to. If I'm in a lesson, I tend to be quite formal. Often teachers try to make us talk in full sentences and explain our ideas in detail. Sometimes they correct us if we don't use grammar properly or use slangy words when we should use formal ones. I can be a lot more relaxed with my friends and we use a lot of slang. Sometimes we use slang words that have come from multimodal forms, like 'lolling' means laughing and comes from the abbreviation 'lol' meaning 'laugh out loud'.

Now read what an examiner has said about this piece of work.

This student is working at Level 6 because he is beginning to explore how different things influence the way he speaks. He is picking out clear and appropriate examples to back up his points.

- Produce your own piece of writing called 'My Idiolect Try to suggest reasons for why you talk the way that you do, rather than just giving examples.

Checklist for success

✓ Write between 200 and 250 words.

✓ Use the extract above as a model.

✓ Use the information about yourself from the table in *Getting you thinking* to give you ideas.

✓ Give some examples of how you talk differently in different situations.

Check your level

LEVEL 5	I can explain features of my own idiolect and those of other speakers.	
LEVEL 6	I can explore in detail features of my own idiolect and those of others.	
LEVEL 7	I can analyse features of many idiolects clearly and suggest a range of factors which influence them.	

3 Attitudes to spoken language

Learning objective

- To explore different attitudes to spoken language.

Bridge to GCSE

- At GCSE, one of the key areas of study is 'social attitudes to spoken language'. This can mean what different groups of people think about particular ways of speaking and how these attitudes change over time or vary in different places.

Many people have strong opinions about the 'correct' way of speaking. In some situations, we can look down on people for not speaking formally enough; in others, we can criticise people for being too 'posh'. Your friends, families and teachers will probably have different opinions about the way you speak.

This is an important area of study at GCSE. You can look at why different social groups speak in different ways and how the way we speak can help to give us our identity. You can also explore why some forms of speech seem to have higher status than others.

Getting you thinking

Rebecca is a 14-year-old girl who lives in Chelmsford. This is what she said about having an Essex accent:

> I suppose I've got an Essex accent. I don't mind because most of my friends speak like I do and I wouldn't want to get rid of my accent because they'd all think I was trying to be posh or something. I think other people look down on my accent and think you're a bit stupid or common if you've got a strong Essex accent. The media makes this worse most of the time and there are lots of jokes about Essex girls going round all the time. I think my mum is very aware of this: she uses a different voice when she answers the phone until she knows who she's talking to and she's always telling me to stop dropping my aitches and to pronounce my 'T's properly. It gets on my nerves sometimes but I think my mum doesn't want other people looking down on me even though I can speak formally when I need to.

In groups, discuss Rebecca's account, then read the questions below. Prepare a short presentation to give to the class. If people in the group have different opinions or experiences, make sure to include these in the presentation.

1 What do people think about your accent/dialect? Do they view it positively or negatively?

2 How do you feel about your accent/dialect? Does it make you proud? Is it part of who you are?

3 Does everyone in your year group speak in the same way? What do you think other students in your year group think about the way you speak? Do you have any views or opinions on the way other people in your year group speak?

4 Do you have the same accent and dialect as your friends?

5 What do your parents think about the way you speak? Is your accent stronger, less strong or different from theirs? Do they correct you or encourage you to speak differently?

6 What do your teachers think about the way you speak? Do they ever correct you or encourage you to speak more formally?

GCSE skills focus

Oscar-winning actress Emma Thompson stirred up controversy in the media when she talked about a visit to her old school in an interview with the *Radio Times*. Here's what she said:

Key terms

Articulacy Being able to express oneself clearly and concisely, using meaningful words.

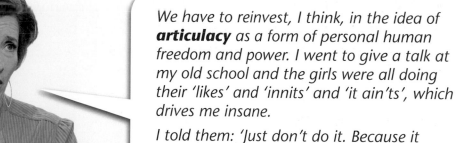

*We have to reinvest, I think, in the idea of **articulacy** as a form of personal human freedom and power. I went to give a talk at my old school and the girls were all doing their 'likes' and 'innits' and 'it ain'ts', which drives me insane.*

I told them: 'Just don't do it. Because it makes you sound stupid and you're not stupid.'

There is the necessity to have two languages – one that you use with your mates and the other that you need in any official capacity.

Rapper and comedian Doc Brown responded to Emma Thompson's comments in a discussion about slang in *The Observer*:

My initial response is that slang may indeed 'sound stupid' if heard out of context or removed from its natural habitat. But I can guarantee a lovely bit of RP (**Received Pronunciation**) will sound pretty stupid at 3.45 pm on the basketball court on my estate. As with all forms of language, there is a time and a place for slang. It is worthy, even vital, in some arenas, useless in others.

So who are these people that transfer slang from the courtyard to the classroom? Outside of my career in music and comedy, I have worked with teenagers in songwriting workshops for nine years now. My last job was for Southwark Council with eight boys all fresh out of Feltham on knife charges, and every one of them naturally switched their patter to 'correct' English when addressing me and other staff (monosyllabic at times, but correct!).

Thus, from my own experience, I would question your fear of young people continuing to use slang in the formal world. If a person is idiotic enough to use slang in a job interview, for example, I would have thought the last thing the employer should worry about is the way that person speaks!

Key terms

Received Pronunciation
Sometimes described as the 'Queen's English' or 'BBC English', this is what some people would consider as 'speaking properly' and others would consider as 'speaking posh'.

Now you try it

Imagine you are being interviewed for a news report wanting to find out teenagers' views on this issue. Working in pairs (one as interviewer, one as teenager) role-play the interview. You could use these questions or think of your own:

1 Who do you most agree with, Emma Thompson or Doc Brown? Why?

2 Why do you think some older people look down on younger people for using slang?

3 Why do you think young people use slang?

4 What might happen if you use the wrong kind of spoken language for the context?

5 Do you think young people are subject to peer pressure and use slang just to 'fit in'?

6 Do you think it would be better if everyone spoke Standard English with an RP accent? What would be the advantages and disadvantages?

What have you learnt?

In pairs, evaluate your role play using the *Check your level* box below.

Ask yourselves:

● How much detail did you go into when explaining the views of Doc Brown and Emma Thompson?

● Could you suggest reasons why they might hold those views?

● Could you come up with alternative viewpoints of your own and justify them?

● Did you show a clear understanding of terms like RP, Standard English and slang?

Check your level		
LEVEL 5	I can explain a range of different attitudes to spoken language.	
LEVEL 6	I can explore different attitudes to spoken language and make appropriate comparisons.	
LEVEL 7	I can analyse and suggest reasons for different attitudes to spoken language and evaluate them.	

Understanding context

Learning objective

- To explore why some registers are more formal than others.
- To start to look at analysing significant details in a transcript.

Bridge to GCSE

- At GCSE you will need to comment in detail on specific examples of language use. This may sometimes involve commenting on a transcript of a conversation or speech.

In this lesson, you will explore the skills necessary for analysing a transcript. You will think about how the context influences the way people speak and identify specific examples to back up your ideas. You will learn how to comment on your examples in detail rather than just spotting techniques.

Getting you thinking

One way we can alter the formality of our register is through the vocabulary we use.

1 Look at these ways of describing discontent and rank them in order from **most formal** to **least formal**:
- gutted
- fed up
- disenchanted

2 Find three more synonyms for each of the following terms and rank the terms from **most formal** to **least formal**:
- happy
- good-looking
- food
- tired
- friend
- embarrassed.

GCSE skills focus

Read the following transcript. The underlined words show when the speakers are talking simultaneously (at the same time).

> **Female 1:** do you like my new skirt, <u>does it look</u>
> **Female 2:** <u>it's right nice</u> (.) is it from New Look
> **F1:** it were only fifteen and I thought it weren't going to fit but it did (.) and it don't make me look too fat (.) does it
> **F2:** don't be (.) don't be silly <u>there isn't no fat on you</u>
> **F1:** <u>your hair</u> looks nice (.) <u>did I tell</u>
> **F2:** <u>oh thanks</u> (.) yours does too (.) what were you saying sorry
> **F1:** did I tell you about what happened <u>on sat</u>
> **F2:** <u>no what</u>
> **F1:** well you know about the thing with <u>jasmine</u>
> **F2:** <u>yeah</u>
> **F1:** well you will never guess what happened
> **F2:** what <u>happened</u>
> **F1:** <u>so</u> (.) so (.) they only had a massive argument on the street
> **F2:** oh no (.) on the street (.) poor jas
> **F1:** yep on the street (.) and she stormed off

Key:
(.)   short pause
—   interruption or simultaneous speech

To help you understand the transcript, think about:

- whether the speakers are male or female
- how old both speakers are
- whether the speakers know each other very well.

In an analysis, if you can describe the context of the speech, you can more easily explain if and why speakers are using informal or formal registers.

Top tip

The context is the first thing that will give you a clue as to how formal or informal speech is.

You could make points like:

- The topics are social and not very serious because the speakers are friends: for example, discussion of clothing, hair, Jasmine's argument with her boyfriend.

To be sure of Level 5, you would then give a specific example and explain it:

- F2 shortens Jasmine's name to 'Jas'. This is something friends do all the time.

Now you try it

Analyse the transcript using the following prompts:

- The two speakers are comfortable with each other because they use informal language like...
- The two speakers are obviously friends because...

Give examples from the extract to back up what you are saying and try to explain each example clearly.

What have you learnt?

Highlight where you have included and explained evidence from the transcript.

- If you have done this clearly you will have achieved Level 5.
- If you have gone into detail in some of your explanations of key points in the transcript you are moving towards Level 6.

Check your level

LEVEL 4 I can show that I understand how speakers change the way they speak in different situations.

LEVEL 5 I can explain how and why speakers change the way they speak in different situations and give examples.

LEVEL 6 I can explain how and why speakers change the way they speak and explore examples in detail.

5 Analysing a spoken genre

Learning objective

- To extend your understanding of the conventions of a particular genre of speech: sports commentary.

Bridge to GCSE

- At GCSE, you may choose to look at a particular spoken genre in detail and learn about the conventions of that genre.

In this lesson you will analyse and evaluate a specific spoken genre: sports commentary. You will identify conventions of this genre and develop the ability to evaluate and reflect on how these are used by real commentators, with some live examples.

Getting you thinking

Commentary is the real-time description of events by a commentator to a listening or viewing audience.

Commentary is most often associated with sport but is also used to accompany live news events.

- Working with a partner, see how many other events or situations you can think of where commentary is used.

- Then, as a pair, decide what the purpose of commentary is:

  a on the radio

  b on TV.

GCSE skills focus

The conventions of commentary are outlined in the following table.

Convention	Example/Reason
Vocabulary	
Use of slang, especially metaphor and cliché	It really is a *game of two halves* Lampard has a terrific *engine*
Use of jargon	Federer's *sliced backhand* skids off the court
Prosody	
Changes in tone, pitch and volume	GOOOAALL! THAT'S UNBELIEVABLE! …the brave soldiers of the Scots Guards file silently past the cenotaph…
Fluency	
Commentary generally proceeds at a steady rate with few or no pauses	Radio commentary has almost no 'dead air' TV commentary has few pauses
Often uses a cyclical or 'loop' structure with 'colour' added in between loops	Tennis proceeds in points Guests appear individually or in small groups at premieres, with gaps in between
'Expert' guests often join commentators	A former player gives his/her views on the action

Convention	Example/Reason
Grammar	
Adverbials used widely (adverbials are adverbs or phrases that help to explain how something is done)	Gerrard places the ball *carefully* and *deliberately* on the spot I'm cooking the steak *quickly on a high heat*
Present tense used	Ennis *starts* her run-up, *pulls* the javelin back and *launches* it. *That's* a good throw.
Use of omission and ellipsis (missing out words which the listener has to imagine)	Murray serves to backhand. Nadal cross-court. Forehand down the line from Murray. Back down the line from Nadal's forehand. Drop from Murray. Into the net.
Use of extra modifiers	Collingwood, *England's 'Brigadier Block'*, keeps out another inswinger from Mitchell Johnson, *the left-arm Aussie quick*.
Use of passive voice (the subject comes after the verb)	And the shot *is blocked* by... Matthew Upson. He put his body on the line there.

Now you try it

Look at this transcript. It is a short excerpt from the TV commentary to a horse race: Thirsk 14.55 Hambleton Cup Handicap. Stuart Machin is commentating for Channel 4 Racing.

and Brouhaha is in all set and they're off they jump for the Hambleton Cup over a mile and a half Kames Park red jacket a little slowly away as is so often the case with him and the short-priced favourite Green Lightning towards the inside prominent just about leads River Ardeche from out wide in the noseband crossing over to keep Green Lightning company through the first furlong tracked by Ethics Girl in the black and yellow Lady Luachmhar often takes quite a pull in her races and she races quite keenly in fourth George Adamson in the noseband races in fifth and then back to Brouhaha Snow Dancer and a couple of lengths to Kames Park

Answer the following questions:

1. How can you tell Stuart Machin is commentating on a fast-moving sport? How does he help the viewer keep up?

2. What examples of specialist language or jargon can you find?

3. Find some examples of ellipsis and suggest reasons why Stuart Machin uses it.

4. This is a fast-moving commentary on a fast-moving sport. How might the commentary on a slower sport, such as cricket, be different?

4 Now read the next two sections or 'loops' of commentary. What is the reason for the loops or cycles? What features does each loop contain?

as they swing the turn away from packed enclosures on Lady's Day as Green Lightning a well-supported favourite here seeking to make all in the hands of Sylvester De Sousa tracked by River Ardeche Ethics Girl close up and Lady Luachmhar still racing a little freely George Adamson the red white and blue still sitting in fifth place racing just in advance of Snow Dancer as they start off down the far side Snow Dancer preceded by Brouhaha Kames Park remains at the tail

they've completed four and a half furlongs and Green Lightning at his own gallop really not given too much pressure by River Ardeche

Taking it further

Now look at this transcript from the Sky Sports TV commentary on the game between MK Dons and Hartlepool from 4 September 2010. It comes from the first three minutes of the second half. The score is 0-0 and the match has been quite uneventful.

Bill Leslie

Key:
(.) short pause
(2) (3) two, three,
(5) (7) five or seven second pause
[...] gesture/noise
___ overlapping speech

Commentator (Bill Leslie): nil-nil the scoreline at full time when these two met here last season [whistle – second half starts] still forty-five minutes for the side from Buckinghamshire or the side from the northeast to do something about it (2) and MK Dons attacking their preferred cowshed in this second half – that's the end of this gleaming new stadium where their home supporters are housed.

Expert (Garry Birtles): we certainly saw that they had the ability the invention and craft to unlock defences, MK Dons – just that final ball let them down but also we saw the problem that [loud crowd noise – inaudible] created

Commentator: here's Easter finding himself some space which is closed down by Hartlepool (.) Chadwick (2) just overran it, Humphreys collects Boyd (.) Humphreys spinning it with the outside of his boot looking for the run of Yantorno (.) one of two South Americans we've got on show here Yantorno the Uruguayan in the orange of Hartlepool and the Colombian Balanta playing wide on the left for MK Dons [goalkeeper kicks ball long] (7) on by Humphreys [ball out for throw-in] (2) he certainly had one of the stand out efforts in the first half for Hartlepool (.) great drive which he [throw-in taken] hit just wide (5)

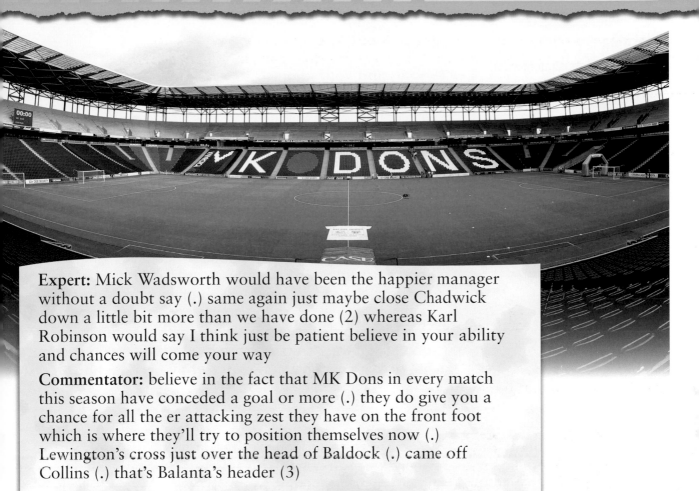

Expert: Mick Wadsworth would have been the happier manager without a doubt say (.) same again just maybe close Chadwick down a little bit more than we have done (2) whereas Karl Robinson would say I think just be patient believe in your ability and chances will come your way

Commentator: believe in the fact that MK Dons in every match this season have conceded a goal or more (.) they do give you a chance for all the er attacking zest they have on the front foot which is where they'll try to position themselves now (.) Lewington's cross just over the head of Baldock (.) came off Collins (.) that's Balanta's header (3)

Make notes on this transcript using information from the table on pages 168–169. Try to focus on:

- highlighting or identifying specific examples
- commenting on the effects of, or reasons for, specific examples of language use
- how the transcripts are examples of their genre and how well the commentators do their jobs.

What have you learnt?

Look back at your work on the two transcripts in this section. Read the level descriptors from the *Check your level* box to assess your current Level for spoken language.

Check your level

LEVEL 6 I can analyse my ideas with close focus on specific examples.

LEVEL 7 I can explore a range of possible interpretations and evaluate them.

LEVEL 8 I can analyse in detail and reflect on how examples fit the conventions of a spoken genre.

Learning objective

- To investigate strategies for researching spoken language.
- To explore how to analyse research effectively.

Bridge to GCSE

- At GCSE, doing your own research may well be more enjoyable than analysing a text given to you by your teacher. Also, knowing the context of what you are analysing may help with your analysis.

You have a choice of two tasks:

1 Analysing your idiolect

Earlier in this chapter you thought hard about your own use of language. You can use all that research now. However, you need to be careful to avoid just describing features of your idiolect. You have to analyse. Keep asking yourself why you speak like you do and why other people view your idiolect the way they do.

2 Analysing a spoken genre – sports commentary

For this assignment, you could use the horse racing or football examples on pages 169 and 170. However, you may feel that you can find better examples yourself, especially if you have a keen interest in another sport. To do this, you will need to record an example and transcribe it carefully. You don't want to end up with too much, but you do need to check that your final transcript gives you enough to analyse.

GCSE skills focus

When you are writing an analysis, you need to show understanding of the spoken language you are analysing. You need to be able to pick out specific details and then comment on them in as much detail as possible. You need to be able to write a 'lot about a little' rather than a 'little about a lot'.

1 Analysing your idiolect

Read the question in the box below.

What are the significant features of my idiolect and how do they relate to specific examples of my spoken language?

Checklist for success

✓ Clear introduction: Where are you from? What other context about you do we need to know?

✓ What is your accent and dialect? How do people in general view it? When do you use or not use dialect words?

✓ Do you adapt the way you speak in different situations? When do you use more formal language? When do you use less formal language? Why?

✓ Do you speak differently from your parents? Grandparents?

✓ Conclusion: What is typical or not so typical about the way you speak for someone of your age and location?

2 Analysing a spoken genre – sports commentary

Read the question in the box below.

> *How does your chosen transcript reflect the conventions of sports commentary?*

Checklist for success

✓ Clear introduction: What transcript have you chosen to analyse? Give any other relevant context. What are the key features or conventions you would expect to find in your type of transcript?

✓ What significant details can you pick out? Refer back to the table on pages 168–169. Go through your examples and explore and reflect on them in detail.

✓ Conclusion: How far is your example typical or not so typical of its spoken genre?

Plan your response

Use the checklists to make a plan for your chosen analysis.
You need to pick a few examples to show that you can:

- explain (Level 5) – give reasons for specific uses of language

- explore (Level 6) – give a range of reasons for specific uses of language

- analyse (Level 7) – explain in detail how significant language features work

- reflect on (Level 8) – fit analysis into the bigger picture or wider context.

Write your response

Highlight the three best examples in your plan that will allow you to write a 'lot about a little'. Stay really focused on exploring these examples as you write your analysis.

Reading and reflecting

Learning objective

- To reflect on your analysis of spoken language by evaluating other students' work.

Bridge to GCSE

- At GCSE you will learn to reflect on your own work and evaluate it against grade descriptors.

Look at this extract from Richard's assignment: 'My Idiolect'

I have lived in Norfolk all my life and I get fed up with the way people view my accent. A lot of people think we are all yokels and a bit slow. When I go to Norwich City games, the away fans chant things about 'combine harvesters' and 'tractors'. There are a lot of farms in Norfolk but there are lots of other jobs too. My mum works in an office and my dad's a plumber. They both want me to do well at school and get a good job. I want to go to university and be a physiotherapist.

My parents correct me sometimes when I drop my aitches or use 'was' instead of 'were', but they forget that I'm only doing this because I'm with my friends and would talk differently if I was in a formal situation like an interview. My granddad has a broad Norfolk accent and uses lots of dialect words and my mum's accent gets broader when she is with him. Maybe that's because she used to talk more like that when she was a girl.

> Good comment on social attitudes to his dialect; could suggest reasons as to why these attitudes might exist

> Comments provide useful context, but do not explore how this has shaped his idiolect

> Some examples provided here, but could go further and suggest why his parents might be trying to correct him

> It would be interesting to have some examples here and explore this point. Why might his grandad have a broader accent than his mum?

> This is good: Richard is suggesting a reason for his mum's changing register

Examiner comment:

Richard is working at Level 5 because he has identified and explained some features of his idiolect.

Look at these extracts from Mina's analysis of the football commentary on page 170.

Football commentary does more than report objectively on the action of a match. Commentators add colour and excitement and their purpose is to entertain as much as to inform. In this transcript there is little action on the pitch and the commentator and expert work as a team to keep the audience entertained and, therefore, watching their channel.

> Opening sentence sets out clear thesis and signals understanding of the wider significance of the genre

> Purpose of the commentary is clearly identified and goes on to analyse how features relate to this purpose (suggests Level 8)

The commentator and expert have different roles but work together as a team. Bill Leslie provides real-time commentary on the action as well as statistical information, ('0-0 here last season') and more general colour, ('gleaming new stadium'). Garry Birtles's role as the expert is to focus on the more technical aspects of the game from an insider's point of view – he is a former player. For example, Birtles is more likely to use jargon, as when he states 'just maybe close Chadwick down a little more' using closing down to mean giving a player less time to decide what to do when he has the ball.

> Clearly sets context which will help when explaining details

> Clear topic sentence introduces main idea of paragraph. The rest of the paragraph evaluates the roles of the two speakers in detail (Level 7)

They work together skilfully to keep the level of excitement high – especially when there is little action. After the ball was 'hit just wide' there is a five-second pause. Leslie has nothing to add so Birtles fills the dead air by discussing how the managers are likely to have evaluated the first half. Leslie echoes and extends Birtles's opinions in his next speech with 'believe in the fact that MK Dons in every match this season have conceded a goal or more', repeating the word 'believe' and reinforcing the idea that goals will surely come soon.

> Exploration of how the speakers work together with close analysis of details. (Level 7/8)

Examiner comment:

Mina has focused very closely on specific details and has explored and explained significant features of the transcript. She has also begun to reflect on how what the commentators say is typical of that particular spoken genre. Mina is working at a high Level 7 and, at times, Level 8.

● Now you have looked at these two examples and the examiner's comments, is there anything you could do to improve your own analysis of spoken language?

Check your progress

In this chapter you have considered some differences between written and spoken language. You have also identified and commented on the conventions of different types of spoken and multimodal language using the correct technical terms. You have explored how speakers alter the way they speak to suit different contexts, purposes and audiences. You have undertaken research independently and practised writing to analyse spoken language.

Taking it further

Read the points under each Level heading below. Which Level do you think you have reached in this chapter, and what do you need to do to improve?

LEVEL 5 (Aiming for GCSE C/B)

AF3   I can explain features of my own and others' language use, showing understanding of the effect of varying language for different purposes and situations.

LEVEL 6 (Aiming for GCSE B/A)

AF3   I can analyse the meaning and impact of spoken language variation, exploring significant details in my own and others' language.

LEVEL 7 (Aiming for GCSE A/A*)

AF3   I can evaluate the meaning and impact of a range of significant features of language variation in my own and others' language.

Next steps to GCSE

For GCSE, you will be applying these skills in a controlled assessment. You will have one task to complete where you research your topic independently or use materials provided by your teacher. In the written part of the controlled assessment, you will write an analysis of your data. You will have to be clear about how you are going to analyse your data before tackling the written part of the controlled assessment.